T0316505

Cambridge Elements ≡

Elements in Second Language Acquisition
edited by
Alessandro Benati
The University of Hong Kong
John W. Schwieter
Wilfrid Laurier University, Ontario

INTERACTION

Jennifer Behney
Youngstown State University

Susan Gass
*Southeast University, Nanjing, China
and Michigan State University*

CAMBRIDGE
UNIVERSITY PRESS

University Printing House, Cambridge CB2 8BS, United Kingdom

One Liberty Plaza, 20th Floor, New York, NY 10006, USA

477 Williamstown Road, Port Melbourne, VIC 3207, Australia

314–321, 3rd Floor, Plot 3, Splendor Forum, Jasola District Centre, New Delhi – 110025, India

103 Penang Road, #05–06/07, Visioncrest Commercial, Singapore 238467

Cambridge University Press is part of the University of Cambridge.

It furthers the University's mission by disseminating knowledge in the pursuit of education, learning, and research at the highest international levels of excellence.

www.cambridge.org
Information on this title: www.cambridge.org/9781108792608
DOI: 10.1017/9781108870627

First published 2021

A catalogue record for this publication is available from the British Library.

ISBN 978-1-108-79260-8 Paperback
ISSN 2517-7974 (online)
ISSN 2517-7966 (print)

Interaction

Elements in Second Language Acquisition

DOI: 10.1017/9781108870627
First published online: September 2021

Jennifer Behney
Youngstown State University

Susan Gass
Southeast University, Nanjing, China and Michigan State University

Author for correspondence: Susan Gass, gass@msu.edu

Abstract: This Element in the Cambridge Elements in Second Language Acquisition series examines the role of interaction in Second Language Acquisition research, with a focus on the cognitive interactionist approach. The Element describes the major branches of the field, considering the importance of conversational interaction in both the cognitive interactionist framework as well as in sociocultural approaches to second language learning. The authors discuss the key concepts of the framework, including input, negotiation for meaning, corrective feedback, and output. The key readings in the field and the emphases of current and future research are explained. Finally, the authors describe the pedagogical implications that the cognitive interactionist approach has had on the teaching of second languages.

Keywords: interaction, input, output, negotiation for meaning, feedback, attention

ISBNs: 9781108792608 (PB), 9781108870627 (OC)
ISSNs: 2517-7974 (online), 2517-7966 (print)

This Element is dedicated to the memories of
Teresa P. Pica,
whose early work in interaction influenced our understanding of what
happens in interactions,
and
Michael H. Long,
a giant in the field of interaction-based research
whose foundational work brought us to where we are today.

Contents

1 What Are the Key Concepts?

1.1 Introduction

We begin this Element by explaining why studying interaction is important to an understanding of how second language learning takes place. We do so while at the same time acknowledging that interaction represents only one approach to second language acquisition (SLA). There are many perspectives aimed at accounting for the underlying principles of SLA, the interactionist perspective being just one of them. It is an approach that is important to a broader understanding of what is involved when a nonprimary language is learned. We won't provide detail on other ways of approaching the study of SLA, as they have been outlined elsewhere (e.g., Gass et al., 2020; VanPatten et al., 2020) and in other Elements in this series.

So, what do we mean by an understanding of how learning takes place? VanPatten et al. (2020) provide a discussion of *theory* in relation to SLA. In fact, the title of their book is *Theories in Second Language Acquisition*. Yet, on closer inspection, of the ten chapters that are focused on SLA, five have theory in their title, two have approach in the title, one has model, and two state only the topic. VanPatten et al. define theory as "a set of statements ('laws') about natural phenomena that explains why these phenomena occur the way they do" (p. 2). They further note (p. 4) that theories "ought to account for and explain observed phenomena and also make predications about what is possible and what is not." Models, on the other hand, do not *explain* but, rather, only describe. In their general discussion, VanPatten et al. introduce the concept of a hypothesis that "does not unify various phenomena; it is usually an idea about a single phenomenon" (p. 5). We raise these issues as background to what is now known as the *interaction approach* (Gass & Mackey, 2020, p. 192), the subject of this Element. But referring to it as an approach is a change from the original conceptualization in which it was referred to as the *Interaction Hypothesis*; we return to this later in this Element. Gass and Mackey make this clear: "[F]ollowing a significant amount of empirical work leading to greater specificity and theoretical advancement, it is now generally referred to in the literature as *the interaction approach*" (p. 192, emphasis in original). In other words, it has gone beyond a hypothesis.

1.2 What Do We Mean by Interaction?

Simply put, interaction, in the context of SLA, refers to conversations in which at least one participant is a second language learner, in other words, a nonnative speaker (NNS) of the language being learned, and another participant who is a native speaker (NS) or even another NNS. To understand this better, we begin with a few examples.

In Example 1.1 (McDonough & Mackey, 2006), the second language learner asks a question in English, but the question is not grammatical. The NS repeats the question, but modifies it so that it is a grammatically correct question. This is presumably perceived by the learner as a correction and she modifies her speech accordingly. But the question is: Did she just repeat what the NS said or did she really understand what the response was intended to do, which is to correct an incorrect question?

Example 1.1

Learner:	When it happen?
NS:	When did it happen?
Learner:	When did it happen?

In Example 1.2 (McDonough & Mackey, 2006), there is a similar repetition of an incorrect form, but, in this case, the learner shows that she has indeed incorporated the response by now using the correct question with a new verb.

Example 1.2

Learner:	Why he hit the deer?
NS:	Why did he hit the deer? He was driving home and the deer ran out in front of his car.
Learner:	What did he do after that?

Example 1.3 (Mackey, 2002, pp. 389–390) demonstrates a lengthy exchange in which the NNS is struggling with a new word, *magnifying glass*. This exchange is based on a picture that the NNS is describing to the NS.

Example 1.3

NNS:	And in hand in hand have a bigger glass to see.
NS:	It's err. You mean, something in his hand?
NNS:	Like spectacle. For older person.
NS:	Mmmm, sorry I don't follow, it's what?
NNS:	In hand have he have has a glass for looking through for make the print bigger to see, to see the print, for magnify.

NS: He has some glasses?

NNS: Magnify glasses he has magnifying glass.

NS: Oh, aha, I see, a magnifying glass, right that's a good one, ok.

Following this brief conversation, the NNS was asked what he was thinking about during the exchange. His response was the following:

> In this example I see I have to manage my err err expression because he does not understand me and I cannot think of exact word right then. I am thinking thinking it is nearly in my mind, thinking bigger and magnificate and eventually magnify. I know I see this word before but so I am sort of talking around around this word but he is forcing me to think harder, think harder for the correct word to give him so he can understand and so I was trying. I carry on talking until finally I get it, and when I say it, then he understand it, me.

Thus, it appears that this exchange was useful for vocabulary learning.

The exchanges in the above examples are known as interactions and form the basis of the interaction approach. In short, there is an error, there is correction (feedback), there is negotiation, and there is output following the correction.

It is important to understand that interactions such as these, which are claimed to result in learning, occur not only between NSs and NNSs but also between two NNSs. We present Examples 1.4 and 1.5 (Gass & Varonis, 1989, pp. 80–81) to illustrate this. In Example 1.4, Hiroko and Izumi are describing a picture (Hiroko is describing it to Izumi). Hiroko uses the incorrect preposition *to* and Izumi immediately corrects it (*at*), after which Hiroko immediately modifies her speech.

Example 1.4

Hiroko: Ah, the dog is barking to—

Izumi: At

Hiroko: At the woman.

In Example 1.5, the interaction is a bit longer. The same two participants appear to be unsure of what the correct form is. In the first utterance, we see many instances of hesitation (*uh*) which might suggest that Hiroko is unsure of the accuracy of her speech. But then Izumi responds with a "correction" of the possessive pronoun (*his*) rather than the preposition (*in/on*). And Hiroko, probably recognizing that there is still a problem, comes up with the correct form of the preposition and the possessive pronoun. They both affirm the correctness.

Example 1.5

Hiroko: A man is uh drinking c-coffee or tea uh with uh the saucer of the uh uh coffee set is uh in his uh knee.
Izumi: In him knee.
Hiroko: Uh on his knee.
Izumi: Yeah.
Hiroko: On his knee.
Izumi: So sorry. On his knee.

In sum, the interactionist approach within the SLA literature focuses on exchanges involving second language (L2) learners in which there is an error (in grammar, in pronunciation, in vocabulary) followed by correction of some sort. What happens after the correction is the central part of learning.

1.3 What Are the Main Constructs?

The main constructs involved in interaction-based research are input, (corrective) feedback, and (modified) output. In this section, we also deal with other constructs – intake, negotiation for meaning, and noticing – as they will become important in discussions in later sections.

1.3.1 Input

The definition of input is a simple one referring to the "ambient" language that a learner is exposed to. If we think about input broadly, we can see that there are many ways that exposure to language can come about: language spoken to a learner, language a learner hears (e.g., TV, movies, or the language in the environment if the learner is in a location where the target language is spoken), language a learner sees (in the case of sign language), language in print form (e.g., books, newspapers), and language provided pedagogically such as by a teacher or in a textbook. There is nothing controversial about the need for input for language learning; what is controversial is the type of input needed.

Krashen (1977) and elsewhere described the need for **comprehensible input**. By this he means language that pushes a learner toward acquisition because it is beyond a learner's current level of grammatical knowledge. He argues that providing input that reflects current knowledge is of little value. Similarly, providing input that is way beyond what a learner knows is not useful. For example, if a learner is struggling with simple sentences, such as *I am happy*, then providing input regarding a complex question, such as *Do you know why that little boy is not happy?*, is likely to be of little practical value because it is too far beyond that learner's ability to understand.

Gass (1988) emphasized the need for **comprehended input**, namely, input that the learner has understood. She argued that a crucial difference between the two is who controls the input and what happens after exposure. In the case of comprehensible input, it is the input provider who controls what the input is; in the case of comprehended input, it is the learner who has control of the input in the sense that she has to work to understand all aspects of the input.

The term comprehension has come up in this discussion. There are many ways that one can think of comprehension, the most common being in terms of meaning. If someone says to a learner *The tree is being chopped down by a woman* (assuming an understanding of the meaning of each word), it is likely that the learner will have a general idea that a woman is doing something to a tree. However, comprehension can be at the level of grammar, with a learner understanding the component parts of the sentence, including, for example, word order. Thus, comprehension at the level of meaning can involve not only language but also information about the real world. Even though the object noun *tree* appears before the verb, which is a less common construction in English sentences (objects generally follow rather than precede nouns in English), in this case real-world knowledge helps with the meaning (women can chop down trees, but trees cannot chop down women).

1.3.2 Feedback

Feedback is the cornerstone of the interaction approach. We can think of it as a reaction or a response to an utterance. It is what can alert a learner to a problem with some form of what she has said. We return to this construct in more detail in Section 3, but for now we note that there are many different ways that feedback can occur. We limit ourselves here to oral corrective feedback, but do note that feedback indicating a problem can be provided through facial expressions (e.g., a puzzled look) or deliberate gestures (Nakatsukasa & Loewen, 2017). They can be very explicit or quite subtle. Example 1.6 shows an explicit type of feedback and involves metalinguistic information (Ellis et al., 2006, p. 353).

Example 1.6

Learner:	He kiss her
Researcher:	Kiss—you need past tense.
Learner:	He kissed

Recasts are defined as reformulations of an incorrect utterance while at the same time maintaining the original meaning. Look at Example 1.7 (Ellis et al., 2006, p. 353) where the researcher recasts the learner's initial error (*follow*) with the correct form *followed*.

Example 1.7

Learner:	. . . they saw and they follow follow follow him
Researcher:	Followed
Learner:	Followed him and attacked him.

Yet another subtle way of indicating a problem with an utterance is through elicitation. Elicitation, a form of correction, found more often in pedagogical contexts, does not provide information about the correct form but seeks to elicit the correct form by drawing a learner's attention to the form. In essence, the learner is engaged in self-correction. Example 1.8 (Loewen, 2002) shows this (F is an NNS speaker and T is a teacher). The elicitation occurs in bold where T does not provide a response but attempts to draw a response out of F. Following the initial elicitation, T becomes more specific as to the locus of the problem, but never provides the correct form.

Example 1.8

F:	he is long long time smokert (.) and he's never think about diet (.) he's still going McDonald
T:	**he's he's he's never think?**
F:	he never think of
T:	he's never think is what you said so can you change that
F:	I said
T:	he (laughter)
F:	he () I <could> use never
T:	yeah you could use never

F: he never

T: but rather than think (.) he's never thi- you said he is never think (.) he

F: has ah has ah he ha- he has never (.) thought of giving up smoking

F: good?

T: that's a better way of doing it yeah

F: thank you

In general, feedback can be input-providing or output-prompting (Sheen & Ellis, 2011). In the first, the input can be implicit (as in the case of recasts – see Example 1.7) or explicit (as in the case of a specific correction – see Example 1.6). In the case of output-prompting, the correct form is not provided. These also can be either implicit or explicit. Clarification requests (e.g., *What?* or *I didn't understand*) are an implicit indication that something is wrong and metalinguistic information can be explicit. Considering Example 1.8, when the teacher says "he's never think is what you said so can you change that," he is being explicit as to the source of the error, but does not provide input. Similarly, elicitation is output-providing and, as it indicates where an error has occurred, relatively explicit.

Why is interaction important? Ellis (1984, p. 95) answers this clearly:

> [I]nteraction contributes to development because it is the means by which the learner is able to crack the code. This takes place when the learner can infer what is said even though the message contains linguistic items that are not yet part of his competence and when the learner can use the discourse to help him/her modify or supplement the linguistic knowledge already used in production.

Sato (1986) similarly argued that conversation in and of itself can facilitate grammatical development.

1.3.3 Output

The importance of the role of output was noted by Swain (1985) and elaborated. Her original 1985 paper which had the words *comprehensible output* was, in part, a reaction to Krashen's *input hypothesis*. We return to this concept in Section 3, but in essence Swain argued for the importance of language production (output) as part of learning. In her 2005 paper, she describes the output hypothesis thus: "[T]he act of producing language (speaking or writing) constitutes, under certain circumstances, part of the process of second language learning" (p. 471). Modified output is an outgrowth of the original output hypothesis and includes the idea "of being pushed toward the delivery of a message that is not only conveyed, but that is conveyed precisely, coherently, and appropriately" (p. 473). An example of modified output was seen in Example 1.3 and another can be seen in Example 1.9 (from Mackey et al., 2010). The * in this example from a learner of Spanish indicates an error.

Example 1.9

NNS: necesita *doble a la derecha
       'you need *turn to the right'
NS: necesita . . .?
       'you need . . .?'
NNS: necesita doblar a la derecha
       'you need to turn to the right'

In Example 1.9 we see an elicitation that resulted in the NNS changing the incorrect *doble* to the correct *doblar*. Further discussion of output can be found in Section 3.

1.4 Other Constructs

In this section we deal with other constructs that are important in an understanding of the role of interaction in learning. We have opted to highlight the following: intake, negotiation for meaning, and noticing.

1.4.1 Intake

We have talked about input as the ambient language, or the language to which one is exposed, but some of the input may be incomprehensible and is, therefore, not particularly useful for learning. Early on, Corder (1967) distinguished between input and intake, the latter of which Corder referred to as language that is taken in, that is, internalized. There are many times when we are in a second language environment (either where the language is spoken or even in a classroom) and we are unable to make any sense of what we hear (hence the expression *It's all Greek to me*, which is applicable in many instances unless you understand Greek!). In these situations, we hear sounds and don't even know where one word begins or ends. Intake can be thought of as a subset of what we are exposed to.

1.4.2 Negotiation for Meaning

Negotiation for meaning (also referred to as negotiation of meaning) is a term frequently used to describe interactions such as the one presented in Example 1.3 where the two participants are working toward an understanding of what the other is saying. It can be thought of as a process that occurs during a conversation in which the participants go through an exchange in order to reach an understanding of what the other has said. Negotiation includes asking for clarification, asking your interlocutor to repeat what they said, or even asking for confirmation that you have understood. We elaborate in Section 3.

1.4.3 Noticing

Noticing, another construct, is crucial to understanding the functions of the various component parts of an interaction. Schmidt (1990, 1993a, 1993b, 1994) brought to the attention of SLA research the importance of noticing and attention in understanding the underlying cognitive dimension of the interaction approach. In short, Schmidt and Frota (1986) reported on Schmidt's own learning of Portuguese; Schmidt documented his learning, showing, in particular, how noticing helped in his subsequent learning of new forms.

Negative evidence and positive evidence are terms generally used in the generative literature to refer to information that learners (adults or children learning their first language) receive as they create a language system. Positive evidence is essentially input – in other words, it is the language available to language learners as they are developing their language systems. Negative evidence is information provided to learners that indicates that their utterance has been deviant in some way. This is essentially what we have been discussing when we have dealt with corrective feedback.

We can summarize with the following three figures. In Figure 1.1, the learner receives input (*He flies to Rome*), but the output (*He fly to Rome*) is different from the input. There is corrective feedback (*He flies to Rome*), after which the learner understands the scope of the correction and modifies their speech accordingly.

In Figure 1.2, the learner notices that there is a discrepancy between what she said and what her interlocutor said, but she doesn't understand what the problem was and, hence, makes no modification.

Finally, in Figure 1.3, the learner doesn't notice that there is any mismatch and repeats the malformed utterance.

Figure 1.1 Learner notices correction and makes modification

Figure 1.2 Learner notices correction, but doesn't know what to do with it

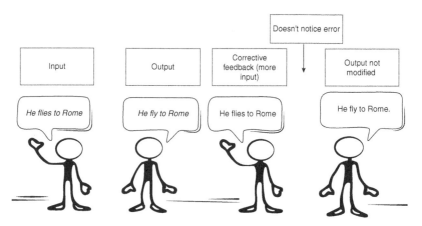

Figure 1.3 Learner doesn't notice correction

1.5 Conclusion

In this section we have covered some of the main constructs used in investigating interaction. We move to a discussion of research directions in Section 2.

2 What Are the Main Branches of Research?

Within the field of SLA there have been numerous research orientations. Some are cognitively oriented and focus on how learners represent and process language; others have a social orientation and are concerned with the context in which learning takes place. These have, unfortunately, been seen as opposing views without much room for overlap and/or complementarity. As Hulstijn et al. (2014) state, the division "runs the risk of disintegrating into irreconcilable approaches" (p. 361). This division has spread to the field of interaction as well. In this section, we first discuss general issues relating to differing orientations and then lay out the main tenets of both approaches as they relate to interaction. In other parts of this Element, we focus on the cognitive-interactionist approach given the expertise of the authors.

Cognitive orientations to SLA focus for the most part on linguistic and cognitive issues, attempting to understand how language is represented and how learners process language. Sociocultural approaches take social activity as central to knowledge (language or otherwise). In other words, the latter views language learning (first and later language learning) as a social endeavor rather than as purely cognitive. The two approaches not only differ in their philosophical underpinnings but also typically diverge in the methods used to investigate and analyze them, with the former often using quantitative and the latter qualitative methods. This Element is not the time or place to delve into the issues of this divide or to even question whether the divide is real. However, we do consider interaction as a place where there is common ground. The phenomenon under investigation is the same (how learning takes place when interaction occurs); it is the explanations that differ.

As a general statement about interaction, Rudd and Lambert (2011), with regard to first language acquisition, state the following, which is a neutral description, in our view, of the role of interaction: "The interaction theory recognizes that both environmental and biological factors are important in language development. ... [A]ll interactionists believe that language acquisition occurs as a result of the natural interaction between children and their environment, more specifically, their parents or caregivers" (p. 830).

As further common ground, both perspectives take interaction as the starting point. However, for cognitive interactionists, interaction is one source of input, and whether or not there is an innate system that propels learning is not an issue.

For sociocultural interactionists, learning takes place in a social context and does not involve an innate system.

Within the context of interaction as a sociocultural phenomenon, Rudd and Lambert (2011) provide the following description:

> [I]interactionists believe that language is a byproduct of children's social interactions with the important people in their lives. Vygotsky [1962] believed that children developed thought and language by actively interacting with adults. He stated, 'The child's concepts have been formed in the process of instruction, in collaboration with an adult' (p. 191). Like Vygotsky, interactionists believe that language develops as a natural consequence of these interactions and that it progresses to more complex levels as the interactions mature. The more mature interactions provoke more complex language structures from parents and caregivers, and this cycle continues until children's language and social skills reach adult levels (pp. 830–831).

2.1 Sociocultural Approaches in Second Language Learning

As was probably clear from the above quote, Vygotsky (1978, 1987) was a leader in the development of what has come to be known as sociocultural theory. The general theory is not a linguistic theory or a theory of language development. Rather, it is a psychological theory whose goal is to understand all sorts of development. In general, all learning is social. Storch's (2017) succinct description is useful. The theory

> explains how biologically endowed mental capacities (e.g., memory, involuntary attention) develop into uniquely human higher order cognitive capacities (e.g., intentional memory, voluntary attention, planning), over which humans . . . can exercise control. The underlying premise in SCT [sociocultural theory] is that the development of these higher order cognitive capacities occurs in contextualized interactions between an expert member of the community (e.g, an adult, a knowledgeable peer) and a novice (e.g., a child, a less knowledgeable peer) (p. 70).

She further points out that "cognitive functions appear first in social interactions between humans, and that they subsequently become internalized within the individual" (p. 70).

Within the field of SLA there have been a number of influential works extending Vygotsky's theory of human development to a second language context, most important being the works by Lantolf and his colleagues (e.g., Aljaafreh & Lantolf, 1994; Choi & Lantolf, 2008; Frawley & Lantolf, 1985; Lantolf, 2012, 2014; Lantolf & Thorne, 2006, 2007; Lantolf et al., 2016; Lantolf et al., 2020). There are principles that are unique to sociocultural theory and that appear only within this framework. First, interaction that results in learning is carried out by a learner and someone with greater knowledge. The ultimate goal is for the more knowledgeable person (perhaps a teacher) to make the learner independent and able to perform linguistic tasks independently. Second, a central construct is *mediation*, which is essentially a tool needed to complete an action. Language is a tool used in thinking and a tool that connects our physical self to the social context around us. Third, as we develop our linguistic skills, we learn to regulate them. In a second language context, our linguistic knowledge is often regulated by others (e.g., a textbook, a computer program, a teacher); with time and increased knowledge, we are able to self-regulate and need little or no support, as is the case with highly proficient speakers. Linguistic knowledge in later stages is internalized and does not need the assistance of an "expert."

As a way of understanding how language mediates thinking, Swain (2006) introduced the concept *languaging*, which she defines as a "process of making meaning and shaping knowledge and experience through language" (p. 98). Languaging can occur in any language and in any modality (writing, signing, speaking) and can be an internal process (known as private speech) or between individuals (collaborative talk). Collaborative talk is different from meaning negotiation, which was discussed in Section 1 in that negotiation of meaning occurs when there is a problem or a communication breakdown. *Languaging* or collaborative talk occurs when there is a problem to be solved; the resources of both participants are drawn upon. Swain (2000) defined collaborative dialogue as "dialogue in which speakers are engaged in problem solving and knowledge building" (p. 101). It is in such dialogues that "one or both speakers may refine their knowledge or come to a new or deeper understanding of a phenomenon" (p. 1). Language is being used to mediate their own thinking as well as that of their partner. Meaning is being coconstructed and leads to learning.

We illustrate this in Example 2.1 from Swain (2000) in which two students use "language as a cognitive tool to mediate their own thinking and that of others" (Swain & Watanabe, 2013, p. 1). They go on to describe what happens in the following way: "Speaking produces an utterance, a product … that can be questioned, added to, discredited, and so forth. This action of co-constructing meaning is collaborative dialogue, and is a source of language learning and development" (Swain & Watanabe, 2013, p. 1). The dialogue in question occurs between two students (English native speakers, grade 8) whose task it was to recreate in French, their L2, a written story based on pictures. They are working on the second half of a sentence whose meaning is "while she combs her hair and brushes her teeth"; the first part of the sentence was *Yvonne se regarde dans le miroir* (Yvonne looks at herself in the mirror …).

Example 2.1

Kathy:	Pendant . . . qu'elle brosse les cheveux.
	(while she brushes her hair)
Doug:	Et les dents.
	(and her teeth)
Kathy:	Non, non, pendant qu'elle brosse les dents et . . .
	(No, no, while she brushes her teeth and . . .)
Doug:	Elle se brosse . . . elle SE brosse.
	(She brushes . . . she brushes [emphasizes the reflexive pronoun])
Kathy:	Pendant qu'elle se brosse les dents et peigne les cheveux.
	(While she brushes her teeth and combs her hair)
Doug:	Ya!
Kathy:	Pendant qu'elle . . . se brosse . . . les cheveux, I mean, no, pendant qu'elle se PEIGNE les cheveux.
	(While she . . . brushes . . . her hair, I mean, no, while she COMBS her hair)
Doug:	Ya.
Kathy:	Et se brosse . . .
	(And brushes . . .)
Doug:	Pendant qu'elle SE peigne les cheveux et SE brosse les dents.
	(While she combs her hair and brushes her teeth [emphasizes the reflexive pronouns])

They eventually end up with a correct French ending to the sentence, but throughout they work together to figure out which verb and noun go together and what the appropriate reflexive form is. In other words, does *brosse* go with *dents* or *cheveux*? Does *peigne* need to have the reflexive *se* or not? Specific to this dialogue, Swain argues that "[t]hrough dialogue they regulate each other's activity and their own . . . Together their jointly constructed performance outstrips their individual competencies. Their dialogue represents 'collective cognitive activity which serves as a transitional mechanism from the social to internal planes of psychological functioning' (Donato, 1988, p. 8)" (Swain, 2000, p. 111).

2.2 Zone of Proximal Development

One other construct that is important is the Zone of Proximal Development (ZPD). (For a more complete understanding and description of sociocultural theory, see the works mentioned earlier in this section.) Vygotsky (1978, p. 86) defines the ZPD as "the distance between the actual developmental level as determined by independent problem solving and the level of potential development as determined through problem solving under adult guidance or in collaboration with more capable peers." It refers to current linguistic capacity and future capacities. In Section 3 of this Element, we discuss feedback and, in particular, the issues surrounding its effectiveness. As a preview, there is controversy surrounding the type of feedback that is effective and the timing of feedback. However, within sociocultural theory, feedback type is based on a learner's current state. Aljaafreh and Lantolf (1994) proposed levels of regulation based on the amount of help needed by a learner. They point out (p. 468):

> Help provided by a more experienced member in a joint activity is designed to discover the novice's ZPD in order to offer the appropriate level of assistance and to encourage the learner to function at his or her potential level of ability. The purpose here is to estimate the minimum level of guidance required by the novice to successfully perform a given task.

Thus, development takes place with appropriate types of assistance (feedback). Greater development is seen in those who can avail themselves of the assistance provided. To exemplify how assistance/feedback is tailored to an individual, Aljaafreh and Lantolf (1994) provide data from students of English enrolled in a language class at a US university. The data come from tutorial sessions. The first example (Example 2.2) is from a Spanish speaker and the next (Example 2.3) from a Portuguese speaker. The same error occurs, but the two need different levels of assistance. In sociocultural terms, different levels of regulation are needed to resolve the issue.

Example 2.2

  Spanish speaker (T=tutor; St=student)

T: Okay in this, okay, "Although I was preparing my travel to USA, with some time almost always we have something to do in the last." Do you . . . is there . . . do you see anything wrong here in this line here? "Although I was preparing myself . . ."

St: I don't know!

T: Okay, "Although I was preparing . . . travel to USA" okay aah

St: long travel

T: Okay, you say "preparing my . . ." instead of travel . . . what's a better word to use?

St: Trip

T: Okay

St: Is better trip?

T: Okay. Yeah "preparing my trip," okay. There is also something wrong with the article here. Do you know articles?

St: Articles, yes

T: Yeah so what's . . .

St: eeh on my trip to . . .

T: What is the correct article to use here?

St: Isn't *to* is . . . no . . . eeh . . . article?

T: What is the article that we should . . .

St: *It*

T: No. Article . . . you know the articles like *the* or *a* or *an*

St: The trip . . . my, is not my? no . . . the trip?

T: My . . . yeah it's okay, you say my trip

St: My trip

T: Okay

St: to United States

T: Yeah USA, what article we need do use with USA?

St: *a, an, the*

T: the, which one?

St: but *the*?

T: Okay, do we use *the* . . . ah preparing my trip to . . . *the* USA?

St: aaah ah (utters something in Spanish) ah okay when I use when I use USA use with article

T: Okay

St: The

Example 2.3

     Portuguese speaker (T=tutor; St=student)

T: "In the same day I mailed them . . . to . . ." okay alright. What about also . . . is there something else still in this sentence?

St: To the

T: hum?

St: The

T: Okay, "to the" . . . yeah, "to the US."

As Aljaafreh and Lantolf (1994) explain when describing the Portuguese speaker, "the learner is very close to being able to control the feature by herself"

(p. 474). In looking at the exchange between the teacher and the Spanish student, greater regulation was needed. It took explicit information to focus on the error.

Storch (2017) reminds us of the term *scaffolding* that originated in work by Wood et al. (1976). Scaffolding is support provided that allows a learner (in the case of Wood et al., a child) to achieve a particular goal. Learning is like a building under construction (Storch, p. 71). She refers to an interesting metaphor, comparing the construction of a building to learning.

> The scaffold is vital for the construction to take place, but it is a temporary structure. As the construction progresses, the scaffold is gradually dismantled and it is removed when the building can stand alone. In education, scaffolding should also be perceived as an important temporary structure. It enables the learner to perform a task beyond their current capacity, but it should be gradually dismantled in line with the learner's increasing expertise and removed when it is no longer needed; that is, when the learner can complete the task independently (p. 71).

2.3 Interaction Hypothesis

The second research strand related to interaction is what was first known as the Interaction Hypothesis, as was noted in Section 1, and what is now more appropriately known as the *interaction approach*. Whereas sociocultural theory had a clearly social orientation, the interaction approach is cognitive in its orientation. It also seeks to understand what it is about an interaction that leads to learning, and focuses on psychological constructs such as attention and noticing, as discussed in Section 1. Emphasis is placed on the type of feedback provided and how that feedback in and of itself triggers language learning.

In Section 3, we will present more detail on the original underpinnings of the Interaction Hypothesis, but for our purposes in this section, we note that an early statement within this tradition comes from Wagner-Gough and Hatch (1975) who argued for the important role of conversation in learning, and not just in practice. Earlier views saw conversation as a venue for practice. Wagner-Gough and Hatch flipped this view and presented data that showed learning taking place within the context of conversation. Ellis (1984) framed the importance of interaction in the following way:

> [I]nteraction contributes to development because it is the means by which the learner is able to crack the code. This takes place when the learner can infer what is said even though the message contains linguistic items that are not yet part of his competence and when the learner can use the discourse to help

him/her modify or supplement the linguistic knowledge already used in production (p. 95).

A decade later, Long (1996) formulated the Interaction Hypothesis, furthering the notion that interaction is a basis for language development. He provides the following explanation as to how this happens:

> [N]egotiation for meaning, and especially negotiation work that triggers *interactional* adjustments by the NS or more competent interlocutor, facilitates acquisition because it connects input, internal learner capacities, particularly selective attention, and output in productive ways. (pp. 451–452)
>
> It is proposed that environmental contributions to acquisition are mediated by selective attention and the learner's developing L2 processing capacity, and that these resources are brought together most usefully, although not exclusively, during *negotiation for meaning*. Negative feedback obtained during negotiation work or elsewhere may be facilitative of L2 development, at least for vocabulary, morphology, and language-specific syntax, and essential for learning certain specifiable L1–L2 contrasts. (p. 414)

The underlying claim is that when there is some form of negotiation, learning is promoted because through feedback (correction of production), a learner's attention is directed to a gap in knowledge. In other words, there is a mismatch between what a learner produces and what a more proficient speaker produces. There are times when learning actually takes place at the moment of the interaction, as we saw in Section 1 (Example 1.3) with the *magnifying glass* example. But, as Gass (1997, 2018) argued, a specific interaction may not be the actual locus of learning, but may serve as a *priming device,* whereby something is noticed and the learner is primed for future learning; in other words, the actual interaction readies the learner for future learning. In this view, conversation is a catalyst for later learning. Two examples illustrate later learning rather than an immediate response.

Example 2.4 (Gass & Varonis, 1989) comes from a picture-description task in which two NNSs are involved. At the beginning of the exchange, NNS1 mispronounces the word *cup.* NNS2 questions what she is talking about and it is this questioning that likely prompts her to question her own pronunciation, as can be inferred by her *Hmm hmmm* response. The conversation continues (seventeen turns) and at the end she correctly pronounces *cup.* Thus, the initial feedback in which NNS2 questioned her word likely focused her attention on the correct pronunciation. She received more input during those seventeen turns and at the end she recognized her original mispronunciation and modified it.

Example 2.4

NNS1: Uh holding the [kʌp].
NNS2: Holding the cup?
NNS1: Hmm hmmm . . .
       [seventeen turns later]
NNS2: Holding a cup.
NNS1: Yes.
NNS2: Coffee cup?
NNS1: Coffee? Oh yeah, tea, coffee cup, teacup.
NNS2: Hm hm.

Example 2.5 is also a conversation between two NNSs.

Example 2.5

NNS1: When will you **get married**?
NNS2: When? I don't know. Maybe . . . uh . . . after thirty.
NNS1: Thirty?
NNS2: Yeah, after thirty **I'll get marriage—I'll get married** . . .
       [three turns]
NNS2: . . . then if I fall in lover with her, I'll **get marriage** with her.
       [eleven turns]
NNS1: And . . . uh . . . when I saw her. I liked **to get married** with a Chinese
       girl because she's so beautiful.

In this example (bolding not in original), NNS1 provides correct input at the beginning of the exchange, namely *get married*. In the fourth line, NNS2 produces the correct form and an incorrect form. It is likely that he thought that the correct form was *get marriage*, since he produced it first, but he is also responding to the input by saying *get married*. The conversation continues and after three turns he still says *get marriage*, but after a rather lengthy exchange, he appears to have made the switch to *get married*. Thus, the original part of the conversation provides the stimulus that allows NNS2 to consider the two forms.

2.4 Looking at Two Strands

We close Section 2 of this Element by presenting a conversation (Example 2.6) and framing it in two different ways, one from the perspective of sociocultural theory and the second from the perspective of the interaction approach. The conversation, presented in Swain and Lapkin (1998), occurs between two French immersion students in Grade 8 who are performing a jigsaw task in which they are writing a story based on pictures that each has (each participant has half of the pictures). The focus is on the noun *alarm clock* **(bolded here for the sake of convenience)**. The correct French word is réveille-matin. Note that French nouns are either masculine (preceded by *le,* the, or *un,* a, or *du,* of the) or feminine (preceded by *la,* or other forms which are not used in this excerpt). On a multiple-choice pretest, Kim demonstrated her knowledge of the correct word; Rick did not. On a multiple-choice posttest, they both selected the correct word. The numbers in the left-hand column refer to turns in the dialogue.

Example 2.6

2. Kim: On peut pas déterminer qu'est-ce que c'est.
           (One can't figure out what it is.)
3. Rick: **Réveille-matin**
           (Alarm clock)
4. Kim: Et il y a **un réveille-matin** rouge . . . sur une table brune, et **le réveille-matin** dit six heures, et c'est tout.
           (And there is a red alarm clock . . . on a brown table, and the alarm clock says six o'clock, and that's all.)
           [Note: the masculine article is used twice]
           [four turns intervene with Kim using réveille-matin twice and Rick once]
9. Rick: Elle est en train de dormir après que . . . **la rêve-matin** est ancore sonné.
           Et le rêve-matin dit six heures un.
           (She is sleeping after the alarm clock rang again. And the alarm clock says one minute after six o'clock.)
           [Note: the feminine article is used followed by the masculine article]
           [forty-six turns later]
55. Kim: . . . il y a **un réveille-matin**.
           (. . . there is an alarm clock.)
           [Note: the masculine article is used]
56. Rick: **Réveille-matin**?
           (Alarm clock?)
57. Kim: **Réveille-matin**.
           (Alarm clock.)
           [nine turns later]
66. Rick: Se réveille à cause . . . du son . . .
           (Wakes up because . . . of the sound . . .)

67. Kim: **Réveille-matin.**
    (Alarm clock.)
68. Rick: A cause du ...
    (Because of ...)
69. Kim: **Du réveille-matin** qui sonne? Does that sound OK?
    (Of the alarm clock that rings? Does that sound OK?)
    [Note: masculine *du* (of the) is used]
70. Rick: (Or what about ... Jacqueline se lève à cause du ... **du réveille-**
    ... yeah, qui sonne
    (Or what about ... Jacqueline gets up because of the ... of the
    alarm ... yeah, that rings)
    [Note: masculine *du* (of the) is used]
71. Kim: OK. Or you can say **du réveille-matin** or du sonnement **du
    réveille-matin.**
    (OK. Or you can say of the alarm clock or the ring of the alarm
    clock.)
    [Note: masculine *du* (of the) is used]
72. Rick: No, **réveille-matin** qui sonne.
    (No, alarm clock that rings.)
    [twenty turns later]
92. Rick: Sur **la rêv-** ... **rêve-matin.**
    (On the alarm clock.)
    [Note: feminine article is used]
93. Kim: Sur **le réveille-matin** pour arrêter le sonnement.
    (On the alarm clock to stop the ring.)
    [Note: masculine article is used]
94. Rick: **Rêve-matin?**
    (Alarm clock?)
95. Kim: **RÉVEILLE-matin**
    (Alarm clock) [Stresses component meaning "wake."]

Swain and Lapkin (1998) focus on what they refer to as language-related episodes (LREs) which they define as "any part of a dialogue where the students talk about the language they are producing, question their language use, or correct themselves or others" (p. 326; and see Swain & Lapkin, 1995). They provide a general characterization of this dialogue as follows:

> In this collaborative dialogue, we are able to observe change in Rick's use of
> the correct term for "alarm clock." It is not a one-time shift from wrong to

right, but a wavering between alternatives. The source of his learning is not only input, although Kim used "réveille-matin: 17 times during their entire conversation Nor was the source of his learning only output, although it may have been Rick's attempt to write it (turn 56) that focused his attention on his own uncertainty about which term to use. We wish to argue that it is the joint construction of knowledge that resulted from Rick's questioning and Kim's responses that, in part, accounts for Rick's shift from incorrect to correct usage. Here Rick's questions serve as hypotheses and Kim's responses serve to conform or disconfirm them (p. 330).

We turn now to an analysis by interactionist researchers. First, it is important to note that some of the concepts that are used by Swain and Lapkin such as hypothesis testing and confirmation and disconfirmation are also present in an interactionist analysis. An interactionist description would have a different emphasis and would bring in the concept of attention and would not include terminology such as co-constructing knowledge or meaning. An interactionist analysis would refer to the input that Rick was getting in turn 4 with additional input in the intervening turns and an "apparent" confirmation in those turns. The question would likely be raised as to whether or not Rick's "confirmation" by providing the word *réveille-matin* was truly a confirmation, which would entail noticing the form or whether it was just a repetition without noticing that there was a gap in his knowledge. An interactionist would recognize that there was hypothesis testing when, in turn 9, there appears to be uncertainty with the lexical item itself as well as with the gender of that noun. In line 10 additional input is provided about both the lexical item and the gender and this is followed by an apparent recognition and then a confirmation of that recognition. Line 69 is additional input with a comprehension check to make sure that Rick agrees. The gender of the noun and the word itself seem to be understood and then confirmed by Kim and acknowledged by Rick. When Rick changes the noun and the gender in line 92, one can speculate whether his apparent confirmations that preceded were anything but repetition without any awareness that a correction had been made. This is made clearer when Kim follows with a final correction (additional input) which Rick apparently still doesn't get, as evidenced by his last turn. Finally, Kim, with emphasis on *réveille*, may have provided just the right amount of information because Rick on a posttest displayed knowledge of the word. An interactionist would see this conversation as one that draws Rick's attention to an erroneous form through feedback, input, and enhanced input (stress).

In Section 3, we go into greater detail about research within the cognitive-interactionist framework.

3 What Are the Key Readings?

This section takes a more extensive look at the cognitive interactionist approach. We approach it historically beginning with early work that focused on input to learners and continuing with milestones along the way. Section 4 deals with current research and Section 5 with teaching applications.

There have been numerous articles that have appeared over the years as well as book-length treatises on the topic. An early book by Gallaway and Richards (1994) was an edited volume that had child-language acquisition as its main focus, although one article (Wesche, 1994) dealt with SLA. Much of it dealt with child-directed speech. In a book that was published shortly after the Gallaway and Richards book, Gass (1997, reprinted in 2018) focused entirely on SLA. She presents an overview of the relationships among input, interaction, and SLA. In particular, she outlines what interaction is and how it furthers language learning. Mackey (2012) has a similar focus. As she notes in the Preface, the book provides "a thorough and in-depth treatment of the current developments and status quo of the field" (p. vi). The book is organized thematically and provides an excellent overview of many of the topics that are covered in this Element. Ellis (1999) delves into the topic in his book that examines different theoretical perspectives (cognitive and sociocultural) and different areas of language (e.g., vocabulary, grammar). Mackey edited an important volume (2007) which covers a broad range of topics and languages. Other books (e.g., Nassaji & Kartchava, 2017, 2021; Long, 2015; Philp et al., 2013) provide detail on various aspects of components of the interactionist approach, such as task-based language teaching (Long), corrective feedback (Nassaji & Kartchava), and peer interaction (Philp et al.). As in Long, Mackey (2020) relates interaction research to task-based language teaching (Long)/learning (Mackey). She emphasizes three important aspects – namely interaction, feedback, and tasks – in her comprehensive and well-written book on these topics. These are just a sampling of the book-length treatises dealing with the topics. In addition, there have been numerous meta-analyses and overviews of the interactionist approach (e.g., Abbuhl et al., 2018; Gass, 2010; Gass & Mackey, 2006; Gass & Mackey, 2020; García Mayo & Alcón Soler, 2013; Lyster, 2019; Mackey et al., 2012; Mackey & Goo, 2007, Plonsky & Gass, 2011; Sheen, 2010) to which you can refer if interested.

This section is organized around milestones. These are, of course, limited and somewhat subjective; the milestones represent how we see the development of the interaction approach. In essence, this section provides historical background which, we argue, is important in understanding the development of this area of research. We again point out that it is not a comprehensive theory of language; it is one way of accounting for second language development. This was noted nearly a quarter of a century ago by Pica (1996) who, in talking about interactionist research, pointed out that it is compatible with a wide range of theories. In her words, "[a]s a perspective on language learning, it holds none of the predictive weight of an individual theory. Instead, it lends its own weight to any number of theories" (p. 1). Similarly, Mackey (2012), in referring to her 2007 edited volume, pointed out that "interaction can be regarded as a facilitator of many of the processes involved in learning, functioning as a window through which we can view important aspects of development" (p. 4). Finally, Gass (2018), in the introduction to her book where a transcript of an interview with Alison Mackey appears, stated that interaction "is important in learning, but it is not the only contribution to learning and it is in a sense, agnostic, with regard to linguistic theory. It doesn't have a theory of language. It is probably easier to say that it has psycholinguistic underpinnings" (p. xiv).

To briefly recap, the goal of the cognitive interaction approach is to account for learning based on input to the learner (i.e., exposure to language), production of language (i.e., output), and feedback to the learner. An excellent summary is provided by Mackey (2012, pp. 4–5):

> Interaction is argued to provide L2 learners with learning opportunities during exchanges of communicative importance that contain critical linguistic information. The input and output processes involved in interaction are such that the cognitive mechanisms driving learning can be optimally engaged in processing form-meaning relationships in linguistic data. Interaction often involves feedback and modifications of utterances as interlocutors attempt to resolve the misunderstandings sometimes caused by problems with language use. Through interaction, L2 learners are provided with opportunities to notice differences between their own formulations of the target language and language used by their native (NS) and non-native speaking (NNS) conversational partners, and they are sometimes pushed to modify their output in order to be understood.

Thus, through interaction, important information about the language being learned is made available to learners. This is not to say that learners always avail themselves of this information. We return to this point in Section 3.2.1 when we talk about attention and noticing. Note that Mackey used the word "opportunities" and we have used the word "available." Both make it clear that the learner is the one who must do the work to make use of the available opportunities.

We begin with the construct of input and point out that interest in input has had a rocky history in language acquisition research. One can think of behaviorist approaches (e.g., Bloomfield, 1933) in which language learning was viewed as imitation of adult models. Within the behaviorist framework (a framework developed for child language acquisition), a child learns to speak by mimicking and analogizing. A child develops habits by repeating what an adult says (albeit not always correctly) and from this her language grows by analogizing from what she knows or by repeating what has been said. The theoretical stance of behaviorists was carried over into second language learning, most notably by Fries (1957) and Lado (1957) (for a more detailed discussion, see Gass et al., 2020).

With the important work of Chomsky (e.g., 1959), interest in input per se waned as the emphasis turned to internal cognitive mechanisms that were triggered by input. Thus, the input was backgrounded in terms of theoretical importance (see Slabakova et al., 2020 for greater detail on generative approaches to SLA).

But interest in input and the characteristics of input never disappeared, even after Chomsky's emphasis on mental representations and innateness. Ferguson (1971) noted similarities between language addressed to young children and language addressed to second language learners. The first he called *baby talk* (although it also has other names, such as *child-directed speech* or *caretaker speech*); the second was known as *foreigner talk*. Among the characteristics of so-called foreigner talk, we find slower speech, simpler vocabulary, simpler grammar, etc. (see Hatch, 1983, for an extensive coverage of these features).

Another theoretical approach that relies on input as a central construct can be found in usage-based approaches. Input takes center stage in that language learning comes about on the basis of exposure to language and experiences using the language. General cognitive learning mechanisms come into play as learners induce rules of the L2 based on exposure. Ellis and Wulff (2020) explain this as follows:

1. Language learning involves learning of constructions.
2. Learning involves learning the appropriate association between form and meaning.
3. A learner's knowledge is "rational such that a learner's knowledge of a given form-meaning pair at any point ... is a reflection of how often and in what specific contexts the learner has encountered that form-meaning pair" (p. 64).
4. Language learning is mainly implicit (i.e., a learner is not consciously aware of learning).

5. Language learning is gradual and the language system developed by second language learning emerges "from the interaction of simple cognitive learning mechanisms with the input (and in interaction with other speakers in various social settings)" (p. 64).

For further discussions of usage-based approaches in SLA, there are numerous summary works you can refer to (e.g., N. C. Ellis, 1998, 2002, 2006, 2008, 2017; Ellis & Wulff, 2020; Wulff, 2013, 2021; Wulff & Ellis, 2018).

As noted in Section 1, Krashen proposed the input hypothesis as part of what he called the Monitor Model (see Gass et al., 2020, for details). Krashen assumed an innate structure (an acquisition device) that served both first and second language learning. Input of a particular kind activates this device and allows a second language grammar to develop. As briefly mentioned in Section 1, the input that is useful for grammar development is "comprehensible input," which he describes as $i + 1$, where i is a learner's current level of knowledge and $+1$ is the next stage. In Krashen's words (1985), "[w]e move from i, our current level to $i + 1$, the next level along the natural order, by understanding input containing $i + 1$" (p. 2). This, of course, assumes some sort of natural order and also specifies the role of the teacher in a language class. The difficult part would be to determine i for any given student, but if one were able to do that, the task is to provide sufficient quantities of input that represents the next stage. Again, in Krashen's words, "[w]e acquire by understanding language that contains structure a bit beyond our current level of competence ($i +1$). This is done with the help of context or extralinguistic information" (1982, p. 21).

As we mentioned in Section 2, Corder (1967) made an important distinction between input, that which is available, and intake, that which a learner internalizes, thus emphasizing that not all input is used for learning.

But it soon became apparent that input was not enough and we now turn to the next milestone, a milestone that moved the focus away from just input to include an interlocutor's role in the learning process.

3.1 Interaction

We briefly touched upon the work by Wagner-Gough and Hatch (1975) in Section 2. In a sense this was the initial recognition in second language research of the importance of interaction and the role it plays in language learning. They considered "the relationship between speech directed to the learner and his speech production" (p. 297). As noted, they recognized the significant learning function of interaction and considered proposing that grammar development resulted from interaction. They presented data from

Homer, a five-year old child from Iran. In particular, he used what he heard (generally what was addressed to him) in a few ways. Examples include meaning extensions and incorporation. An example of the first is his extension of the phrase *What's this*, something said to him frequently. He used that phrase to serve many functions, as can be seen in Examples 3.1–3.3, taken from Wagner-Gough & Hatch (1975, p. 301).

Example 3.1
Identification
>   What this is Elmer (= This is Elmer)

Example 3.2
Advice/help
>   What this is? (=What should I do now?)

Example 3.3
Command
>   What is it tunnel! (=Stop pushing sand in my tunnel!)
>   What this is Homer! (=I'm Homer and you can't tell me what to do!)
>   What is this this it. (=Give me that truck!)

He also incorporated immediately preceding speech into his own, as in Examples 3.4–3.6 below.

Example 3.4
Mark: Come here
Homer: No come here. (I won't come.)

Example 3.5
Mark: Don't do that
Homer: Okay, don't do that. (Okay, I won't do that)

Example 3.6
Judy: Where are you going?
Homer: Where are you going is house.

Or, there may be intervening speech, as in Example 3.7.

Example 3.7
Ed: Which one?
Homer: I'll show you is that one Which one is that one

To summarize, Wagner-Gough and Hatch (1975) demonstrated the important role that conversation had in the development of linguistic knowledge. Hatch (1978a, 1978b) published two milestone papers dealing with the relationship between interaction and learning in which she essentially flipped the role of conversational interaction. The learning of grammatical knowledge did not necessarily lead to the learner's use of that knowledge in conversation. Rather, she proposed the opposite. Learners learned from conversation.

Another landmark piece in the study of interaction came from Long (1980, 1981). In his seminal work, he took the work of Wagner-Gough and Hatch a step further and looked at characteristics of talk to NNSs and examined the function in terms of language learning. He pointed out that the structure of conversations involving nonproficient NNSs was quantitatively different from other conversations in that there were more comprehension checks, confirmation checks, and clarification requests, examples of which are seen in Examples 3.8–3.10 below.

Example 3.8

Comprehension check
    NNS: I was born in Nagasaki. Do you know Nagasaki?

Here the NNS is checking to see if her interlocutor understands what she is talking about.

Example 3.9

Confirmation check
    NNS1:   And your family have some ingress.
    NNS2:   Yes ah, OK OK.
    NNS1:   More or less OK?

Example 3.10

Clarification request
    NNS1:   When can you go to visit me?
    NNS2:   Visit?

In Example 3.9 NNS1 was attempting to verify that her partner was following her. In Example 3.10 NNS2 doesn't understand the word "visit" and requests clarification.

But, in addition, the actual structure is modified with what he referred to as "or-choice" questions and "decomposition," shown in Examples 3.11 and 3.12, respectively. In the case of "or-choice" questions, it is hypothesized that the question type serves to help the NNS determine what the topic of the exchange is about. In Example 3.12, when there appears to be some difficulty (there is a silence of two seconds after the NS asks the first question), the task is "decomposed," that is, broken into parts by first establishing the topic (that the NNS went fishing in Santa Monica). Having established that fact, the NS can then quite easily ask the relevant question, namely, *When?*

Example 3.11

Or-choice question (Long, 1981, p. 264)
- NS: Aha Do you study?
  Or
  Do you work?
- NNS: No

Example 3.12

Decomposition (Long, 1981, p. 266)
- NS: When do you go to the uh Santa Monica? (2) You say you go fishing in Santa Monica, right?
- NNS: Yeah
- NS: When?

Long documented the frequent uses of these devices in conversations with nonproficient NNSs. In fact, Long (1983a) describes fifteen conversational devices that are used by NSs in conversations with NNSs. "Their use goes some way to making linguistic input comprehensible to the SL acquirer" (p. 138). This is not to say that these do not exist in NS–NS conversations, only that they are less frequent.

Long (1981, p. 270) asked the important question "of whether modified input, modified interaction, or a combination is necessary for or facilitates SLA in a natural or a classroom setting." He further concludes (p. 275) that "while input

to NNS unquestionably is modified on occasion in various ways, it is modifications in interaction that are observed more consistently ... research is needed
that tests the current hypothesis: participation in conversation with NS, made
possible through the modification of interaction, is the necessary and sufficient
condition of SLA." This, in fact, is the precursor to what later became the
Interaction Hypothesis (discussed in Section 2.3) and which we discuss further
in Section 3.2.

Initially, studies were largely descriptive in terms of the structure of
conversations. This was the case with Long's 1980 dissertation study as
well as other studies conducted in the 1980s (Varonis & Gass, 1985a,
1985b; Gass & Varonis 1985, 1989; Pica, 1987, 1988). For example,
Varonis and Gass (1985a) proposed a model to describe what happens in
NNS conversations in such a way as to demonstrate the complexity of these
interactions. In their model, they are able to show how a conversation can be
put on hold while meaning is negotiated. Example 3.13 from Varonis and
Gass (1985a, p. 74) demonstrates a simple example of how conversations are
negotiated. They describe negotiations as consisting of triggers (a grammatical phrase, a lexical item, a pronunciation issue) whereby a problem is first
encountered. This is then followed by some indication that a problem has
arisen, followed by a resolution which can consist of a response and/or
a reaction to the response.

Example 3.13

NNS1:   And what is your mmm father's job?
NNS2:   My father is now retire.
NNS1:   Retired?
NNS2:   Yes.
NNS1:   Oh, yes.

In Example 3.13, the word *retire* is the trigger, as apparently NNS1 doesn't
understand. *Retired* in the next line is her indication of a problem. The next two
lines constitute a resolution to the problem with a response (*yes*) and a reaction
to the response (*Oh, yes*). There are instances elaborated on in their article in
which negotiations are lengthy and build on one another with the result of taking
up the majority of a conversation.

As early research moved forward, there was an initial emphasis on comprehension, that is, on how conversational modifications aid in comprehension. Studies by Gass and Varonis (Varonis & Gass, 1982; Gass & Varonis,
1984) and Long (1983a) considered factors related to comprehension and, in

the case of Long, the effect of adjustments on comprehension and acquisition. Long's argument was that adjustments serve the purpose of helping an NNS understand what is being said (with the assumption that if comprehension didn't exist, there could be no acquisition), and "comprehensible input promotes acquisition" (p. 189). These arguments were an important step in beginning to think about how adjustments (i.e., interaction) ultimately promote learning. Long (1983b) provides a description of fifteen interactional devices that are frequently found in conversations with NNSs. Long (1983c) argues that a conversation is where the NNS (or the less competent speaker) can indicate his/her lack of comprehension and when this happens, there is some negotiation about what is being said. Finally, it is through negotiation that the language becomes comprehensible, with acquisition being a potential result.

We introduce two studies, both published in 1994, that address the relationship between interaction and comprehension (Ellis et al., 1994), on the one hand, and between interaction and production (Gass & Varonis, 1994), on the other. We then discuss a third one (Mackey, 1999) that was also seminal in determining an interaction–learning link.

Ellis et al. (1994) compared the effect of premodified input, interactionally modified input, and unmodified input on vocabulary acquisition. Participants (Japanese learners of English) listened to instructions about where to place objects. One group listened to an unmodified script (derived from a script to NSs), another to a premodified script (derived from a script to NNSs), and a third listened to the unmodified script but were allowed to interact with the teacher who was reading the script. There were a number of important findings. First, there was more input and greater redundancy (determined by the number of repetitions in the input) by the interactionally modified group. In other words, interaction led to more input. The authors calculated comprehension scores, finding that the interaction group comprehended more than the other groups, although it was not just a matter of the frequency of modifications. In addition to looking at comprehension, the authors were concerned with vocabulary acquisition on a posttest and a delayed posttest (approximately one month after the treatment itself). Modified input (whether interactionally modified or premodified) resulted in better vocabulary knowledge on both posttests. When comparing the two modified input groups, the interactionally modified group outperformed the premodified group, though only on the posttest that occurred immediately following treatment; at the time of the second posttest, there were no differences between the two groups. In sum, interactionally modified input leads to greater vocabulary knowledge, and premodified input can also facilitate vocabulary acquisition. Ellis et al.

(1994) suggest "that interaction gives them control over the input they receive and enables them to systematically identify and solve comprehension problems" (p. 481). The important concept of attention is also raised when they state that "learners achieve comprehension because interaction gives them a degree of control over the input they receive and because it buys them time to focus their attention on key or problematic items" (p. 482). We thus see the beginnings of an explanation of the role of interaction in L2 learning.

The second important study that began to investigate the actual relationship between interaction and acquisition is that of Gass and Varonis (1994), who looked not at comprehension but at production. They were interested specifically in the "lasting effects" of interaction and modified input. The task involved an NS–NNS pair in a picture description task in which the NS described to the NNS where to place objects on a board. The descriptions were either modified or unmodified and were obtained in much the same way as the Ellis et al. (1994) scripts. That is, prior to the onset of the actual study, an NS described the picture to another NS, resulting in what was the unmodified script. The modified script was obtained from a recording of an NS describing the picture to an NNS. For the experiment itself, half of the dyads used the modified script and half the unmodified script. Within each group, half of the pairs were allowed interaction and the other half were not. Following this picture description, there was another. In the second picture description task, it was the NNS who described to the NS. Again, half of the pairs were allowed to interact. Figure 3.1 (adapted from their study) illustrates the design.

On the first trial there were fewer errors in placement (i.e., better comprehension) when the script was modified and fewer errors when interaction was allowed (regardless of modified vs. unmodified script). Greatest comprehension occurred

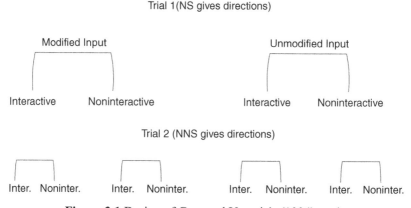

Figure 3.1 Design of Gass and Varonis's (1994) study

when there was a modified script and interaction was allowed. For the purposes of understanding the lasting effects of interaction, it was important to consider the second trial (in which the NNS provided directions). In other words, what differences were there on the second trial based on what the NNS had experienced on the first trial? An initial finding was that whether or not interaction was allowed on the second trial did not seem to affect the success of object placement. But more important was the finding that those NNSs who had been involved in an interactive exchange on the first trial performed better on the second trial, as evidenced by accurate placement of objects by the NS on the second trial. Thus, being able to interact when receiving directions influenced performance when giving directions. The fact of having modified or unmodified input on the first trial did not yield a significant difference on the second trial, although, contrary to expectations, there were more errors on the second trial when the first trial had been modified. Modified input had an immediate effect on comprehension, but not on production. This study was significant in that it was able to show the lasting effects of interaction on production, but it did not demonstrate precisely where the benefits were. The authors had hypothesized that the greatest area to be impacted would be the lexicon, but that did not turn out to be the case. What learners did seem to take from the first trial were descriptive devices rather than linguistic ones. This is seen in Example 3.14.

Example 3.14

	From first trial (interaction allowed)

Jane: All right now, above the sun place the squirrel. He's right on top of the sun.

Hiroshi: What is ... the word?

Jane: Ok the sun.

Hiroshi: Yeah, sun, but ...

Jane: Do you know what the sun is?

Hiroshi: Yeah, of course. Wh-what's the

Jane: Squirrel. Do you know what a squirrel is?

Hiroshi: No.

Jane: Ok. You've seen them running around on campus. They're little furry animals. They're short and brown and they *eat nuts* like crazy.
Second trial

Hiroshi: The second thing will be ... put here. This place is ... small animal which *eat nuts*.

Jane: Oh, squirrel?

Hiroshi: Yeah (laughter)

In concluding their paper, Gass and Varonis (1994) argue for the importance of negotiation because it "focuses a learner's attention on linguistic form, on ways of creating discourse, and, in particular, on ways of describing objects" (p. 298). They further point out that "attention ... is what allows learners to notice a gap between what they produce/know and what is produced by speakers of the L2. The perception of a gap or mismatch may lead to grammar restructuring" (p. 299). They go on to argue that

> interactional input provides a forum for learners to readily detect a discrepancy between their learner language and the target language and that the awareness of the mismatch serves the function of triggering a modification of existing second language knowledge, the results of which may show up at some later point in time. Destabilization, then, is crucial if learning is to progress to higher levels (p. 299).

These ideas had begun to be expressed in previous literature (e.g., Long, 1992: Schmidt, 1990) and serve as the basis of the Interaction Hypothesis, which we discuss in Section 3.2.

The third significant paper in determining the link between interaction and learning is by Mackey (1999). This research was important in that, unlike the Gass and Varonis (1994) study and, to some extent, the Ellis et al. (1994) study, it focused the effect of interaction on a particular grammatical structure. Mackey (1999) asked two central questions: 1) what is the relationship between interaction and second language development and 2) can the developmental outcomes be traced to the actual interaction and to learners' involvement? Her study involved questions in English for which there is an established developmental sequence (Mackey & Philp, 1998; Pienemann & Johnston, 1987; Pienemann & Mackey, 1993; Pienemann et al., 1988; Spada & Lightbown, 1993). The developmental stages are provided in Table 3.1 (from Mackey, 1999, p. 567). Note that Stage 1, which includes only single words or sentence fragments, is not included.

Mackey divided her participants into five groups: 1) those who were allowed interaction and who were at a proficiency level that was sufficiently advanced to allow them to proceed to a higher level of question formation; 2) those who were allowed interaction but who were deemed unready to move to higher levels given their proficiency; 3) a group who observed, but did not participate in interactions; 4) a group that received premodified input, developed in much the same way as in the Ellis et al. (1994) and the Gass and Varonis (1994) studies; and 5) a control group that did not participate in any of the tasks. Important for the development of our understanding of the function of interaction is the fact that conversational interaction did have an important role in

Table 3.1 Question forms and developmental stages

Stage	Description of stage	Examples
2	SVO Canonical word order with question intonation	*It's a monster?* *Your cat is black? You have a cat?* *I draw a house here?*
3	Fronting *WH*/Do/Q-word Direct questions with main verbs and some form of fronting	*Where the cats are?* *What the cat doing in your picture? Do you have an animal?* *Does in this picture there is a cat?*
4	Pseudo Inversion: Y/N, Copula In yes/no questions an auxiliary or modal is in sentence-initial position. In *wh*-questions the copula and the subject change positions	(Y/N) *Have you got a dog?* (Y/N) *Have you drawn the cat?* (Cop) *Where is the cat in your picture?*
5	Do/Aux-second Q-word → Aux/modal → subj (main verb, etc.) Auxiliary verbs and modals are placed in second position to *wh*-questions (and Q-words) and before subject (applies only in main clauses/direct questions).	*Why* (Q) *have* (Aux) *you* (subj) *left home?* *What do you have?* *Where does your cat sit?* *What have you got in your picture?*
6	Cancel Inv, Neg Q, Tag Q (Canc Inv) *Can you see what the time is?* Cancel Inv: *Wh*-question inversions are not present in relative clauses. Neg Q: A negated form of *do*/Aux is placed before the subject. Tag Q: An Aux verb and pronoun are attached to end of main clause.	(Canc Inv) *Can you tell me where the cat is?* (Neg Q) *Doesn't your cat look black?* (Neg Q) *Haven't you seen a dog?* (Tag Q) *It's on the wall, isn't it?*

development. The participants who were actively involved in an interaction (groups 1 and 2) showed evidence of development in two ways. First, they improved more than others in terms of developmental stages and second, they produced more question forms at higher-level stages. Like the other two studies described earlier, this study showed that participating in an interaction had a positive effect on the development of question formation. We present

Example 3.15 from one learner in the interaction group to show a learning trajectory. The first seven lines are from the pretest, the next nine from the treatment consisting of information-gap tasks covering three weeks, the next line is from the first posttest, and the last two are from the second posttest.

Example 3.15

Pretest (stage 3)

> NNS: The meal is not there
> NS: No, it's gone, what do you think happened?
> NNS: Happened? The cat?
> NS: Do you think the cat ate it?
> NNS: The meal is the is the cat's meal?
> NS: It's not supposed to be the cat's dinner. I don't think so. But although this, this cat have eaten it.

Treatment

> NNS: What the animal do?
> NS: They aren't there, there are no bears.
> NNS: Your picture have this sad girl?
> NS: Yes, what do you have in your picture?
> NNS: What my picture have to make her crying? I don't know your picture.
> NS: Yeah ok, I mean what does your picture show? What's the sign?
> NNS: No sign? ... No, ok, What the mother say to the girl for her crying?
> NS: It's the sign "no bears" that's making her cry. What does your sign say? The sign? Why the girl cry?

Posttest 1 (stage 5)

> NNS: What do your picture have?

Posttest 2 (stage 5)

> NNS: What has the robber done?
> NNS: Where has she gone in your picture?

Thus, in this example, the learner started off at stage 3, then, following treatment in which there was significant negotiation, modification, and input, the learner produced stage 5 questions.

Up until this point, we have provided descriptive information about what conversational interaction involving nonproficient speakers looks like and we have also begun to see that there is some evidence of the lasting effect of interaction. The next step is to turn to the "why." What is it about interaction that results in development?

3.2 Interaction Hypothesis

Research on interaction was initially referred to as the Interaction Hypothesis. In its simplest form, it accounts for learning in terms of input (exposure), production of language, and feedback on that production. Ellis (1999) described the main claim: "[E]ngaging in interpersonal oral interaction in which communication problems arise and are negotiated *facilitates* language acquisition. That is, it creates conditions that foster the internal processes responsible for interlanguage development" (p. 4, emphasis in original).

3.2.1 What Is It about Interaction that Facilitates Acquisition?

Gass and Varonis (1989) emphasized the "work" that goes into a conversation that is difficult in that understanding is not automatic and refer to work by Stevick (1976) who "argues that acquisition is facilitated precisely by such active involvement in the discourse since the input becomes 'charged,' allowing it to penetrate" (p. 74). Gass and Selinker (1994) elaborated on this, pointing out that "[t]he charge comes from the hearer and not from the speaker. This difference is perhaps better understood if we ... think of comprehensible input as comprehended input, because the important ingredient is the learner's comprehension, not that the input is potentially comprehensible" (p. 219–220), as is implied by the term comprehensible input.

Pica (1994), in an important review article on negotiation and its impact on learning, concluded that research on interaction and negotiation "illustrates ways in which negotiation contributes to conditions, processes, and outcomes of L2 learning by facilitating learners' comprehension and structural segmentation of L2 input, access to lexical form and meaning, and production of modified output" (p. 493). Pica made the important point that negotiation does not guarantee learning. She pointed to the fact that it is most successful with "lexical items and larger syntactic units" (p. 518). This is discussed in Section 3.4 on learner perceptions. She also considered learner variables, in particular learners' readiness to learn (see discussion in Section 3.1 on the work of Mackey, 1999).

Ellis (1999) noted the importance of what can be referred to as noticing the gap. That is, in some instances of negotiation, a model of correct usage is provided and a learner can match what she said with what her interlocutor said. Ellis (1999) explained it like this: interaction "creates the conditions under which learners can establish links between unfamiliar items in the input and their existing knowledge" (p. 29). (See also Saxton, 1997, who, in the context of child language acquisition, referred to this as contrast theory.)

Long (1996) updated the Interaction Hypothesis by incorporating the important concept of noticing, as developed by Schmidt (1990, 1995). His updated version moves from earlier conceptualizations that emphasized the effect of interaction to an explanation of how interaction works. As noted earlier, at the center of work on interaction is the construct of negotiation, which Pica (1994, p. 494) nicely described as characterizing "the modification and restructuring of interaction that occurs when learners and their interlocutors anticipate, perceive or experience difficulties in message comprehensibility. As they negotiate, they work linguistically to achieve the needed comprehensibility whether repeating a message verbatim, adjusting its syntax, changing its words, or modifying its form and meaning in a host of other ways." As she illustrates, negotiation "can serve as a means of working through perceived or actual gaps in communication" (p. 499), as seen in Example 3.16 from Pica (1987).

Example 3.16

NS: so you came here by yourself or did you come with friends?
NNS: no no I –*what? What you say?*
NS: did you come to the states with friends or did you come alone?
NNS: no, alone_____ from Toronto

In Example 3.16, when the NNS (line 2) clearly does not understand what was said, the NS changes what she probably thought of as somewhat difficult – *by yourself* – to something potentially easier to understand – *alone*. She also elaborates *here* (in the first line) to indicate what it is referring to (*to the states*).

There is one other type of feedback that is common in interaction-based research, namely, what are known as recasts, which we introduced in Section 1. As noted there, they are a subtle form of correction and are not always noticed.

Long (1996) put together the constructs of noticing, attention, and negotiation in his updated version of the Interaction Hypothesis, as discussed in Section 2.3.

As Gass et al. (2020) summarized:

> [T]hrough focused negotiation work, the learner's attentional resources may be oriented to (a) a particular discrepancy between what he or she knows about the L2 and what is reality vis-à-vis the target language or (b) an area of the L2 about which the learner has little or no information. Learning may take place during the interaction, or negotiation may be an initial step in learning; it may serve as a priming device (Gass, 1997), thereby representing the setting of the stage for learning rather than being a forum for actual learning. (p. 434).

Gass and Mackey (2006) illustrated this as shown in Figure 3.2. Essentially, interaction consisting of feedback of different types (i.e., negotiation, recasts) draws attention to what is being corrected and, in an ideal world, results in learning.

More specifically, one might think of the trajectory of feedback as illustrated in Figure 3.3. When feedback is provided, there is the potential that the learner

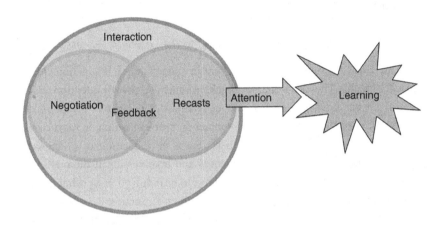

Figure 3.2 A model of interaction (Gass and Mackey, 2006)
Source: S. Gass and A. Mackey (2006). Input, interaction, and output: An overview. In K. Bardovi-Harlig and Z. Dörnyei (eds.), *Themes in SLA Research, AILA Review*, pp. 3–17. Reproduced with the permission of John Benjamins Publishing Company, Amsterdam/Philadelphia, www.benjamins.com.

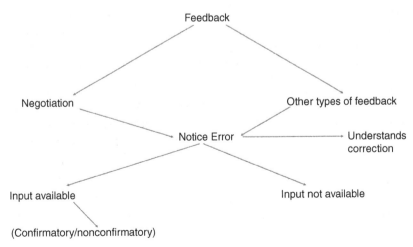

Figure 3.3 The role of feedback

will notice an error. When that happens, learners can either understand the correction or be alerted to a potential issue. At that point, the learner may attempt to verify the correction by paying attention to additional input, after which she may confirm or disconfirm the nature of the correction. Alternatively, there is no relevant input and the learner is left not being able to verify a correction. In that case, the correction may serve as a stimulus to continue looking for relevant data (e.g., in future conversations, in a textbook or dictionary, by asking an NS/teacher).

3.2.2 What Does Interaction Bring to the Learning Process?

There are two constructs that are important in understanding interaction: attention and noticing. The idea is that feedback, in general, draws on attention which "bear[s] on every area of cognitive science" (Allport, 1989, p. 631). Negotiation alerts participants that there is a communication problem which, in most cases, in the context of a conversation with NNSs, is an indication of a language problem. Negotiation requires attentiveness and involvement if there is to be a resolution. In other words, both parties have to be involved in working toward an understanding. Long's (1996) statement, given in Section 2.3, suggests an important role for attention, as does Gass's (1997, p. 132) view that "attention, accomplished in part through negotiation, is one of the crucial mechanisms in this process."

Schmidt (1990, 1993a, 1993b, 1994, 2001; see also Robinson et al., 2012) argued that attention is essential to learning, and even went as far as to claim that there can be no learning without attention. An important study, and one that was the source of Schmidt's research in this area, is by Schmidt and Frota (1986). They reported on Schmidt's learning of Portuguese while in Brazil. For five months, Schmidt (referred to as R) kept a daily journal in which he documented the "most salient aspects of his learning" (Schmidt and Frota, 1986, p. 237). In addition, there were recordings of R in interactions with an NS of Portuguese (S). They documented noticing and later learning of language forms. Example 3.17 shows this, although it focuses on a particular lexical item, whereas in their article they detailed numerous instances of grammatical forms as well. The focus of this example is the word for *wife* in Brazilian Portuguese. The word for *husband* is *marido*, which has the masculine ending *-o*. In many instances in Portuguese, there is a male and a female version of words, so you might think that an obvious way to form the word *wife* would be to add the feminine ending (*-a*) resulting in *marida*; however, in this case it is not correct. The first instance of R's using the word *marida* occurred in their first recording (Example 3.17). S is an NS of Portuguese.

Example 3.17

R: ... e minha ex-marida também professora de inglès.
'... and my ex-wife also English teacher.'
S: ah è?
'oh yeah?'

Later in that same conversation, S uses the correct word for *wife* (*mulher*), which R does not understand (Example 3.18).

Example 3.18

S: A tua mulher, a tua ex-mulher tem descendência oriental?
'Is your wife, your ex-wife of oriental descent?'
R: Hum?
'Huh?'

There are a few exchanges about R's ex-wife's descent that R does not understand (Example 3.19). This is followed by another instance of R's use of the incorrect word.

Example 3.19

R: Non, non. Minha ex-marida?
'No, no. My ex-wife?'
S: É, isso.
'That's it.'

In his journal two weeks later, R referred to S and a transcription of the conversation in Examples 3.17–3.19.

> She told me that ... I've created a word *marida* for wife, when it should be
> *esposa* ... The word I've apparently made up for "wife" astounds me even
> more. Now that the error is pointed out, I see that it is an overgeneralization ...
> I'm shocked because I did that tidy bit of analysis entirely without awareness.
> There are plenty of times when I don't know a word and consciously guess, but
> this is not one of them. I have the strongest feeling, in fact I'm ready to insist,
> that I have never heard the word *esposa*, but I have heard *marida* many times.
> I've been thinking about this all afternoon. S-san [another student] used to talk
> about his wife in class. Didn't he always refer to his wife as *minha marida?*

I guess not, or L would have corrected him. I have a very weird feeling about all this (p. 304).

Over his time in Brazil, R used both *esposa* and *marida* (Example 3.20) but eventually moved more to *esposa*, as he noted in his journal: "At the beach today I said *esposa*. I realized it after, not before I said it" (p. 305).

Example 3.20

R:　　... eu vou lá a Boston, e vou discutir com minha ex-esposa.)
　　　　'... I'm going there, to Boston, and I'll discuss it with my ex-wife.'

Finally, at the end of his stay, R wrote:

> I'm watching TV and just saw a preview of a coming show entitled *Sozinho, marido e mulher,* which clearly means "alone, husband and wife." *Mulher!* No wonder it's been difficult to remember to say *esposa* instead of *marida*. People have not been saying *esposa* unless they have been correcting me. But I can't remember having ever heard people say *mulher* before either, and I'm sure it's not the form people have said I should use. Five months to figure out such a simple thing (p. 305).

Throughout this example, R focuses on the words *marida* and *esposa* and tries to figure out, through feedback and corrections, what the forms are. He also says that he never heard *mulher*; however, when he looks back at transcripts he finds that there were examples used. Thus, just hearing the correct form in the input was not sufficient for learning. He had not noticed the word and even said that he didn't think he had heard it. It took noticing to begin the learning process.

This brings us to Doughty (2003) and Williams (1999) who brought in the concept of memory to account for how learning might take place. Using a mismatch between the input and one's own version of the second language as a basis for learning requires remembering the second language form and making a comparison. We return to working memory and its role in second language learning in Section 4 of this Element.

3.2.3 Interaction in Different Contexts

3.2.3.1 Modality: Computer-Mediated and Face-to-Face Communication

Most research reported up to this point has dealt with face-to-face (FTF) interactions. A separate body has dealt with computer-mediated communication (CMC) (see Cerezo, 2021 for an overview; Ortega, 1997; Ziegler & Mackey, 2017). An important difference between these two contexts is the possibility of eliminating spatial and temporal boundaries. This section compares these two. The issues are numerous and complex and the results are at times conflicting. An early study by de la Fuente (2003) compared these two environments, finding equal benefits with regard to vocabulary learning, but benefits for FTF in oral production. However, as Ziegler and Mackey (2017) pointed out, this may be due to the time limits imposed.

Ziegler (2016) conducted a meta-analysis of interaction in synchronous computer-mediated communication (SCMC). In general, she found an effect for both SCMC and FTF contexts and a slight advantage for SCMC when considering overall outcomes. Measures of production favored SCMC and receptive measures (reading and listening) favored FTF. Other variables considered were 1) physical setting, namely laboratory versus classroom (see Loewen & Gass, 2021 for difficulties in defining these two settings), where a slight advantage for SCMC over FTF was found in both contexts; 2) foreign versus second language settings, where SCMC was slightly advantageous in both; 3) NSs and NNSs, where small effects were found for SCMC for both; and 4) language area, where there was a small advantage for SCMC for grammar and a small effect for FTF for the lexicon. It is important to note that the advantages for SCMC were minimal and led Ziegler (2016) to point out that "mode of communication has no statistically significant impact on the positive developmental benefits associated with interaction" (p. 2).

Affective variables play a role in CMC and FTF interactions. To investigate this issue, Baralt and Gurzynski-Weiss (2011) found no differences in anxiety levels in the two contexts, but Baralt et al. (2016) did find differences in awareness (more so in the FTF context). In addition, attitude was more positive in the FTF environment and, important with regard to interaction, learners engaged more with one another in FTF as opposed to the CMC environment.

Other studies have focused on specific types of non-FTF interaction. In one such study, Saito and Akiyama (2017) considered interaction in video-based contexts. They found that video-based feedback resulted in gains in comprehensibility, fluency, lexical knowledge, and grammatical knowledge, but pronunciation did not benefit. Particularly relevant to an understanding of interaction is Gurzynski-Weiss and Baralt (2014), who did not find significant differences in noticing between the two environments. Another study (Baralt, 2013) considered cognitive complex tasks and interaction in CMC and FTF contexts. Her results suggest an interesting interaction between cognitive complexity and the efficacy of feedback. In the FTF mode, cognitive complexity (operationalized in this study as reflecting on an interlocutor's intentionality during the task) and feedback were more effective than in the CMC mode (where feedback was not effective).

A recent meta-analysis (Cerezo, 2021) considered forty-one studies focusing on written CMC. One conclusion that he came to is that "written SCMC may amplify the developmental effectiveness of corrective feedback in untimed tutor–learner interactions with less complex treatment tasks and formally oriented assessment measures" (p. 511). He also acknowledged that there is disagreement when the two conditions involve peer interaction as opposed to tutor–learner interaction. Even though written SCMC does not yield a greater quantity of negotiation of meaning or form, there is a difference in density when considering negotiation of meaning separate from negotiation of form. In particular, negotiation of meaning is less dense and negotiation of form is more dense.

Ziegler et al. (in press) recently presented an overview on interaction and CMC. Their contribution is not an empirical study that compares learning contexts, but it does point to many benefits that CMC has, including, among other things, providing extra processing time, reducing anxiety, promoting positive attitude, promoting noticing, and increasing possibilities for output. A thorough treatment of technology in SLA is beyond the scope of this Element, but if you are interested, see the forthcoming handbook on this topic (Ziegler & González-Lloret, in press).

3.2.3.2 Second Language and Foreign Language Contexts

Much research in the cognitive interactionist approach was traditionally conducted within a second language environment, that is, in a context in which the language being acquired is spoken by the surrounding community. More recent research has complemented our understanding of interaction and its facilitative effects by examining how it plays out in foreign language (FL) contexts, namely, in countries where the target language is not the language of the community. Alcón-Soler and García Mayo (2009a), in an edited issue of *International Review of Applied Linguistics in Language Teaching*, considered interaction and language learning in foreign language contexts (as compared to second language (SL) contexts) where the importance of context in interaction research was highlighted.

Since the issue edited by Alcón-Soler and García Mayo (2009a), much work has been done considering the differences between FL and SL contexts in interaction. For instance, a fundamental difference between them is the amount of target language input that learners receive and the opportunities they have for interaction, feedback, and modified output (Alcón-Soler & García Mayo, 2009b; García Mayo & García Lecumberri, 2003; Muñoz, 2006; Oliver & Azkarai, 2017; Philp & Tognini, 2009). Learners in an FL setting, for example, may receive only two to five hours of input and opportunities for L2 interaction in the language classroom per week, significantly less than their SL peers who live in an environment in which the language is spoken (García Mayo & García Lecumberri, 2003; Muñoz, 2006; Oliver & Azkarai, 2017).

To add to our understanding of the facilitative benefits of conversational interaction in language development, studies have investigated opportunities for interaction in the FL context (Alegría de la Colina & García Mayo, 2009; Gánem Gutiérrez, 2008; Philp & Tognini, 2009). In addition to learner–learner interaction, teacher–learner interaction has been a frequent focus of FL research, in particular the provision by the teacher of corrective feedback in the FL classroom. Such FL studies of corrective feedback have considered the types of feedback as well as their efficacy and frequency, in terms of elements such as prompts, recasts, and explicit correction (Sheen, 2004; Shi, 2004; Tognini, 2008; Yang & Lyster, 2010).

Other FL research has focused on how the benefits of classroom interaction are affected by task type, task use, and task repetition (Azkarai & García Mayo, 2016; García Mayo & Imaz Agirre, 2016; García Mayo 2002; Gilabert et al., 2009; Oliver, 1995, 1998, 2002). Studies consider traditional FL classrooms, content and language integrated learning (CLIL) classrooms, and immersion classrooms. In CLIL and immersion classrooms, there are greater opportunities for interaction thanks to a greater amount of time spent in the target language.

Use of the L1 in the FL classroom by both teachers and students has been an important area of FL interaction studies. Research has found varying amounts of L1 usage in the FL classroom, by both NS teachers of the target language and teachers who learned the target language as an L2 (Macaro, 2001; Polio & Duff, 1994; Thompson & Harrison, 2014; Tognini, 2008). Likewise, research in FL contexts has considered the purposes of L1 usage in the classroom, including for explaining grammar (Alegría de la Colina & García Mayo, 2009; Macaro, 2001; Tognini 2008; Tognini & Oliver, 2012); for scaffolding as a cognitive or metacognitive tool (Alegría de la Colina & García Mayo, 2009; García Mayo & Lázaro Ibarrola, 2015); for constructing the bilingual identities of the learners and the teacher (De la Campa & Nassaji, 2009; Levine, 2013; Liebscher & Dailey-O'Cain, 2009); and for overcoming communication difficulties (Tognini & Oliver; 2012).

Research in the FL context has furthered our understanding of the benefits of conversational interaction and how such benefits are modulated by opportunities for interaction, provision of feedback in teacher–learner interaction, and use of the L1 in the classroom.

3.2.3.3 Laboratory versus Classroom Context

An important question concerns the ecological validity of research conducted in laboratories. In other words, are the results obtained from laboratory research valid in language classrooms, which are more complex than a controlled laboratory setting. Foster (1998) and later Eckerth (2009) called this into question. In particular, Foster reported data from an English as a foreign language classroom in which negotiated interaction was not prevalent, despite having been prevalent in reports in numerous previous studies conducted, to a large extent, in laboratory studies. Her data included dyads and small groups, as well as different task types. With regard to negotiation for meaning, she argued that it "is not a strategy that language learners are predisposed to employ when they encounter gaps in their knowledge" (p. 1). Gass et al. (2005, 2011) undertook a study to specifically investigate this claim, finding that there were no significant differences between the two settings; however, they did find differences based on task type.

Other studies have had mixed results. Mackey and Goo (2007) conducted a meta-analysis noting first that almost two-thirds of their data were laboratory studies and second, with specific regard to the question at hand, that the impact was greater in laboratory than in classroom settings when measurements were taken on immediate posttests. Another meta-analysis conducted at about the same time (Russell & Spada, 2006) found effects of corrective feedback in both contexts, although that database (fifteen studies in total) was small with 40 percent conducted in a laboratory context. The impact of corrective feedback was strong in both laboratory and classroom settings, but a comparison across contexts could not be made given the small number of studies considered.

Li (2010) also conducted a meta-analysis of lab-based and classroom-based studies of corrective feedback. As with the Mackey and Goo (2007) meta-analysis, a large number (55 percent) of the thirty-three total studies were conducted within a laboratory setting. Different from other studies, he included "small group" (12 percent) studies. He compared the three settings (lab, classroom, small group) and found that there was a greater effect for lab-based over the other two settings.

The studies reported in this section need to be further investigated. Plonsky and Brown (2015) have rightly pointed out that definitions of corrective feedback differ across studies and that the effects of feedback may differ when one considers linguistic areas (e.g., pronunciation, grammar).

3.2.3.4 Age Differences

An important difference in context regarding the role of interaction in SLA is learner age. Child L2 acquisition is distinct from adult L2 acquisition, just as it is distinct from bilingualism, and L2 research on interaction in children has uncovered important differences (Oliver & Azkarai, 2017; Paradis, 2007; Philp et al., 2008). Because of these unique differences, interaction research on child L2 acquisition and the data it provides enrich our understanding of the facilitative effects of conversational interaction. As with research on adults, studies of children have found that they benefit from the facilitative effects of L2 interaction. Child L2 learners provide feedback and negative evidence to their conversation partners, and they respond to that feedback with conversational repair; they negotiate meaning and, in general, benefit from the interaction (Azkarai & Oliver, 2019; Mackey & Oliver, 2002; Oliver, 1995, 1998, 2000, 2002, 2009; Oliver & Mackey, 2003; Pinter, 2006). Studies have also investigated L2 interaction in child–adult dyads (Mackey & Oliver, 2002) or between children and their classroom teachers (Oliver & Mackey, 2003), and have compared the interaction in child–child dyads with that in adult–adult dyads (Mackey et al., 2003; Pinter, 2006).

Although child L2 learners benefit from conversational interaction, important differences have been found in interaction studies conducted with child L2 learners. Mackey et al. (2003) found that child L2 learners actually produce more modified output in interaction episodes than do adult L2 learners. Other studies have indicated that child L2 learners show development from interaction more immediately than adult L2 learners (Mackey & Oliver, 2002; Mackey & Silver, 2005).

Studies in a foreign language context have investigated how child L2 learners negotiate meaning and interact in different instructional settings, for example in CLIL contexts as compared to more mainstream classes (Azkarai & Imaz Agirre, 2016; García Mayo & Lázaro Ibarrola, 2015). Other foreign language context child L2 studies have looked at how variables such as task repetition have an impact on interaction (Azkarai & García Mayo, 2016). Still other studies have examined written corrective feedback among child L2 learners (Coyle et al., 2018; Coyle & de Larios, 2020). Just as child L2 learners have been found to demonstrate differences from adult L2 learners, interaction studies have found differences between younger and older children, for example in terms of task use and task repetition (Azkarai & García Mayo, 2016; Azkarai & Imaz Agirre, 2016; García Mayo & Lázaro Ibarrola, 2015; Oliver, 1995, 1998, 2002).

3.3 Output

The previous sections have focused on input provided to the learner, primarily through interactions. But there is one more area that is central to understanding the role of conversation, and that is output.

The landmark paper in this area is Swain (1985); she later expanded it twice (Swain, 1995, 2005). The title of the paper is revealing: "Communicative competence: Some roles of comprehensible input and comprehensible output in its development." Swain was clearly reacting to the construct of comprehensible input developed by Krashen, arguing that input was not sufficient for language learning. Her observations came from a consideration of children in Canadian immersion programs who after years of "input" were still not at the same level of French proficiency as their NS counterparts. She further observed that their language production was much less. So, the question to be asked is: What does production do that listening and comprehension alone don't? We can think about this by considering what happens in comprehension. When comprehending, we don't need to know the basic intricacies of grammar; vocabulary is often enough (possibly coupled with real-world knowledge) to understand what is being said. Listeners don't have to know basics of grammar such as articles, tense usage, and so forth. On the other hand, language producers have to know a great deal more; knowing vocabulary is not sufficient. Production requires putting words in a particular order, using morphology appropriately, and, among other things, knowing something about pronunciation. Production, then, "may force the learner to move from semantic processing to syntactic processing" (Swain, 1985, p. 249). Swain used the term *pushed output* to refer to learners being pushed to produce language that is comprehensible to others. Being pushed often requires learners to modify their speech.

Being "pushed toward the delivery of a message that is not only conveyed, but that is conveyed precisely, coherently, and appropriately" (Swain, 1985, p. 249) is central to learning. A decade later, Swain (1995, p. 128) further claimed: "[O]utput may stimulate learners to move from the semantic, open-ended, non-deterministic, strategic processing prevalent in comprehension to the complete grammatical processing needed for accurate production. Output, thus, would seem to have a potentially significant role in the development of syntax and morphology."

Swain (1993, pp. 160–161) also suggested that important to learning is the need for learners "to be pushed to make use of their resources; they need to have their linguistic abilities stretched to their fullest; they need to reflect on their output and consider ways of modifying it to enhance comprehensibility, appropriateness, and accuracy." We saw an example of this in Section 1, repeated here for convenience as Example 3.21 (from Mackey, 2002, pp. 389–390). Through the negotiation the learner is pushed to use a new word.

Example 3.21

NNS: And in hand in hand have a bigger glass to see.
NS: It's err. You mean, something in his hand?
NNS: Like spectacle. For older person.
NS: Mmmm, sorry I don't follow, it's what?
NNS: In hand have he have has a glass for looking through for make the print bigger to see, to see the print, for magnify.
NS: He has some glasses?
NNS: Magnify glasses he has magnifying glass.
NS: Oh aha, I see, a magnifying glass, right that's a good one, ok.

In the stimulated recall following this exchange, it is clear that the learner recognizes that he is being pushed to produce the right word because he says (see Section 1) "he is forcing me to think harder, think harder for the correct word to give him so he can understand and so I was trying."

We have seen that pushed output provides an opportunity for learners to reflect on what they are doing and make adjustments, if possible. There are other important roles for output. One is hypothesis testing. That is, in a conversational interaction, learners can try new things and get feedback as a way of determining correctness. How this works can be seen in Example 3.22 (from Mackey, 2002, pp. 390–391).

Example 3.22

Learner A: And then go home
Teacher: And then he goes home?
Learner A: Perhaps he go spaceship holograph room? Suit?
Teacher: Really?
Learner A: And then he goes back to his planet or to suit? . . .
Learner A: Really, he goes home to his planet by the hologram suit.
Learner B: He go home but maybe not realist have house like earth:
Teacher: You mean the holographic suite? The holodeck? Suite? Suit?
Learner A: I mean suite suite hologram suite like hotel
Teacher: You had me really confused. Anyway, it's not his planet he is in the holodeck.

The following is an excerpt from the stimulated recall interview with Learner A in Mackey (2002):

She does not believe that he go back to Earth so she correct me, because she likes to think of his his does not go back to his planet. I am thinking at that time why she say "really?" she understands me or does not agree me or does not like my grammar or my pronounce?, and she does not understand me. Sad for teacher, but XX together we driving her crazy, he joins me and now she thinks there is not chance. But I keep trying and here, here, she finally she gets my meaning, and she corrects me, and I see I am not I do not was not saying it in the correct way, it is suite suite and this sound better, sound correct, even to me (p. 391).

This exchange includes many of the features we have referred to in this Element. For example, there are models provided by the teacher, a recast, and clarification requests. But what is germane to this discussion is the function of hypothesis testing seen when Learner A says "So I try again with the answer she like to hear but I still try out suit, suit, I cannot get the correct word but I see in my picture, written in the door of the room and I think it is a name, name of this area, I say suit, suit, I was try it to see how I sound and what she will say . . .."

A similar example of hypothesis testing, also in the realm of pronunciation, comes from a study by Mackey et al. (2000). Example 3.23 and the following recall comment come from their data, although this particular example did not appear in the final publication. The data came from learners of Italian as a second language who were describing a picture to an interviewer.

Example 3.23

NNS: *poi un bicchiere*
       'then a glass'
INT: *un che, come?*
       'a what, what?'
NNS: *bicchiere*
       'glass'

In the recall data, the learner makes it clear that she was using the conversation as a way to test a hypothesis:

> I was drawing a blank. Then I thought of a vase but then I thought that since there was no flowers, maybe it was just a big glass. So, then I thought I'll say it and see. Then, when she said *"come"* (what?), I knew that it was completely wrong.

Another way that output plays an important role in learning is in the development of automaticity. In earlier views of language learning and teaching, it was believed that grammar rules were presented and a conversation was a forum for practice. In a sense, we can still maintain this view by recognizing the need for repeated use as a way of developing fluency. If we think of the human mind as one with a limited capacity and assume that deliberate tasks require more time and memory, it is clear that creating greater automaticity (less deliberate use of language) is useful in language use. McLaughlin (1987, p. 134) claimed that automatization involves "a learned response that has been built up through the consistent mapping of the same input to the same pattern of activation over many trials." We can see that output builds on the same idea, with learning involving the consistent mapping of grammar (i.e., practice) onto production (output) to give a greater amount of automatic processing.

A third function of output is development of metalinguistic awareness, in particular by providing learners with a forum to notice what they do and don't know, as discussed in Section 1.3.3. Swain (1995, pp. 125–126) made this clear when she said that output allows learners to "notice a gap between what they *want* to say and what they *can* say, leading them to recognize what they do not know, or know only partially" (italics in original).

A final role to mention is the move from meaning-based to grammar-based language use. We noted at the beginning of this section that Swain's initial proposal was that output forces learners to rely more on grammar than on meaning only.

To summarize, through the use of language, learners can test hypotheses and gain feedback, the latter being a way to focus attention on their own language and the potential differences between what they have produced and what an NS or more proficient speaker has produced. The result may be an immediate instance of learning, as in the case of the magnifying glass conversation (Example 3.21), or a moment that is useful as a learner gathers more information (e.g., through additional input, direct questioning, and/or looking in grammar books and dictionaries).

Before moving on to Section 3.4 on perceptions of feedback, we present Example 3.24 to demonstrate the difficulty that a learner may have in interpreting feedback. The context for this exchange is a bakery in central Italy. The NNS wants to purchase pizza and to know when the pizza will be ready.

Example 3.24

NNS: Arriva?
  'Is it coming?'
NS: Sí, è in arrivo.
  'Yes, it's coming.'

The NNS (long experienced in studying interaction) was bewildered. Was what she said an error? Or was the response simply another way of indicating that the pizza was almost done? Spoiler alert: it was an alternative phrasing, not a correction.

3.4 Perceptions of Interactive Feedback

Pica (1994) was perceptive in her understanding that feedback is not always beneficial and is more likely to impact vocabulary and large syntactic units. Mackey et al. (2000) investigated this idea empirically. If the claims that have been made about the value of interaction and, in particular, negotiation are valid, it is important to understand whether learners actually perceive corrective feedback in the way it was intended. Mackey et al. (2000) asked the question: What do learners perceive? They collected data from ten learners of English as an L2 and seven learners of Italian as a foreign language. Each learner was paired with an NS (English) or a fluent speaker (Italian) and involved in a picture-description task. Feedback was provided in morphosyntactic, lexical, and phonological forms. Immediately after the task, the learners viewed a videotape of the interaction and were asked to verbalize the thoughts they'd had at the time of the original inter-actions. Examples 3.25–3.27 show 1) the interactions and 2) the recall comments. In the first, the interview provides feedback on the use of a morphological feature of Italian (gender, plurality), but the learner perceived the feedback as feedback about her word choice.

Example 3.25

Morphosyntactic feedback (perceived as lexical feedback)
> NNS: C'è due tazzi.
>   'There is two cups (m. pl.).'
> INT: Due tazz—come?
>   'Two cup—what?'
> NNS: Tazzi, dove si puó mettere té, come se dice questo?
>   'Cups (m. pl.), where one can put tea, how do you say this?'
> INT: tazze?
>   'cups (f. pl.)?'
> NNS: ok, tazze.
>   'ok, cups (f. pl).'

Recall: "I wasn't sure if I learned the proper word at the beginning."

In Example 3.26, the correction was about pronunciation and the learner accurately understood it to be about pronunciation.

Example 3.26

Phonological feedback correctly perceived
NNS: Vincino la tavolo è.
       'Near the table is' [the correct form is *vicino*].
INT: Vicino?
       'Near?'
NNS: La, lu tavolo.
       'The ? table.'

Recall: "I was thinking ... when she said *vicino* I was thinking, OK, did I pronounce that right there?"

Finally, in Example 3.27, the feedback was about vocabulary and the learner understood the feedback correctly.

Example 3.27

Lexical feedback correctly perceived
NNS: There is a library.
NS: A what?
NNS: A place where you put books.
NS: A bookshelf?
NNS: Bok?
NS: Shelf.
NNS: Bookshelf.

Recall: "That's not a good word[;] she was thinking about library like we have here on campus, yeah."

These examples exemplify the results. Greater accuracy (i.e., a correct match between intention of feedback and understanding of feedback) was noted in perceptions of lexical, semantic, and phonological feedback. Morphosyntactic feedback was where there was the greatest mismatch, supporting Pica's earlier suggestion. To understand this, it is useful to think about the typical focus of a conversation, which is on meaning and not on language. Both phonological and lexical errors are important to understanding; morphological errors, such as are found in an utterance like *The dog bark*, do not interfere with meaning.

Mackey (2002) also considered learner perceptions through interactive dyads and follow-up stimulated recall sessions. In general, there is good news for researchers. There is overlap between researchers' understandings of inter-action and the way that learners understand it. Where Mackey (2002) does find challenges is in her discussion of learner–learner data, representing what typically is found in classrooms. An illustration from her study is given in Example 3.28 (pp. 392–393).

Example 3.28

Learner A:　And here goes er, er, a rule.
Learner B:　A rule? Sorry?
Learner A:　So sorry, a rule like like for distance
Learner B:　rule?
Learner A:　A rule
Learner B:　A tape, like soft or hard?
Learner A:　Hard.

Learner A stated in their stimulated recall session:

> He did not get my meaning of a rule so I have to tell him like a measure so he can understand me. I could try another word like measure but I am not sure it is correct, or how it sound, [measure] [mzure] so also, if I try this he will not understand this so I do not try.

Learner B commented in their stimulated recall session: "I did not follow rule. At that time, I think he means to measure but I am not sure about this word. I wonder how to draw like a tape or like a wood. I do not say measure because I am not sure it will confuse."

Clearly, there was a lack of understanding of the word *rule*. They both understood that the meaning had something to do with measuring, but weren't confident enough to use the word. What this shows is that percep-tions of one's interlocutor's proficiency in the target language and the related understanding about who is and who is not an expert user play into the efficacy of feedback.

Finally, we consider different learning environments (see also Section 3.2.3). Gurzynski-Weiss and Baralt (2014) investigated learner perceptions of feedback in FTF contexts and in CMC. The participants were university English speakers studying Spanish who participated in an information-gap task. Feedback was given when there were errors in vocabulary, morphosyntax, semantics, and phonology (relevant only in the FTF context, with spelling being the "counter-part" in the CMC context). As in the Mackey et al. (2000) paper, there was a stimulated recall session following the interaction. We focus on two of the five research questions posed in their study: 1) Do learners recognize the target of the feedback provided during task-based interaction? 2) Does learner perception of feedback differ according to the mode in which it is provided (i.e., CMC or FTF)? Their results support those of earlier research. In particular, accurate perception was greatest for vocabulary in both conditions. Second was semantics, also in both conditions. Morphosyntax was third. Unlike the Mackey et al. (2000) study, however, phonology was not accurately perceived to a great extent due to the fact that there were few examples. With regard to the mode in which interaction took place, it did not differentially affect the perception of corrective feedback based on language area (e.g., vocabulary, morphosyntax).

3.5 Conclusion

Thus far, we have considered a somewhat abbreviated history of interaction, moving from a description of interactive events to an explanation of why interaction is useful as part of SL learning. In Section 4 of this Element, we move to a discussion of the next step in research on interaction. What is it that makes interaction result in learning and what is it that does not? That is, what are variables that one must think about in a fuller understanding.

4 What Are the Current and Future Research Emphases?

In a sense, the previous sections of this Element have considered interaction in the absence of individual learners. We have made it clear that interactions provide opportunities for learning while also noting that learning is not guaranteed. A question that emerges is, thus: When does interaction result in learning and when does it not? More recent research has looked at individual differences that might lead to successful outcomes. The topics we consider are : 1) aptitude, working memory, and analytic ability; 2) inhibition; 3) anxiety; 4) learner backgrounds (WEIRD populations, literacy, age); and 5) cognitive creativity.

4.1 Aptitude, Working Memory, Analytic Ability

Aptitude has long been considered important to SL research. Many consider working memory capacity and analytic ability to be components of aptitude. A discussion of aptitude goes beyond this Element; what we do in this section is briefly report on current research that addresses aptitude-related issues.

In Section 3 we mentioned the role of working memory, recognizing that when feedback is provided, learners have to retain the information while they attempt to determine that 1) correction has occurred, 2) what the correction is about, and 3) how to modify their output. Working memory research in SLA has had an important role over the past few decades (Linck et al., 2014; Williams,

2012), with some research taking place in the context of understanding who benefits from interaction. Briefly, working memory refers to how humans store and manipulate information. A commonly cited definition comes from Miyake and Shah (1999): working memory consists of "those mechanisms or processes that are involved in the control, regulation, and active maintenance of task-relevant information in the service of complex cognition, including novel as well as familiar, skilled tasks" (p. 450). In other words, it involves one's ability to maintain information in an active state while processing additional information at the same time.

One model of working memory consists of 1) two slave systems (the phonological loop and the visuospatial sketch pad) that regulate a memory system and 2) the overall manager of information (see Baddeley, 2003a, 2003b; Baddeley & Hitch, 1974). The phonological loop, as the name indicates, is where phonological information is stored; the visuospatial sketch map is where visual, spatial, and kinesthetic information is stored. The "supervisor" is referred to as the central executive and coordinates information, particularly in a multi-tasking situation. Baddeley (2000) has suggested a fourth component, what he calls the episodic buffer that integrates information from the two slave systems. We can understand how this works in the context of paying only half attention. Assume that you are in a conversation, but you aren't fully paying attention. Someone asks you a question and you realize that your lack of attention is going to embarrass you. You can often recall what has been asked by having kept the information in storage; however, the information is not stored for long and if you are asked to respond after a delay, you probably will not be able to remember what was asked.

For the purposes of this section, it is important to recognize that working memory capacity differs across individuals. Consequently, the ability to use working memory in interaction varies. How can we understand the individual variation that exists? There are many ways of measuring individual working memory capacity; what is common is the measurement of storage and manipulation, meaning that working memory tasks measure memory and processing. We provide detail on reading-span tasks to give a brief understanding of what is involved, noting that there are many working memory tasks that are used, some verbal and some nonverbal (e.g., using digits). In a typical reading-span task, participants are presented with a sentence on a computer that remains for a predetermined amount of time. Sentences are presented in blocks (usually two to six in a block) after which participants are told to write down the last word of each sentence (in some versions, after each sentence is a letter and participants are told to write down each letter). This is the memory part. An additional element comes from judgments of plausibility after each sentence is presented (e.g., *After the final exams are over, we'll take a well-deserved banana* vs. *Jim was so tired of studying, he could not read another page*). Participants are asked if the sentence is plausible or not. This represents the processing part.

As has become clear, interaction involves hearing information, storing it, and manipulating it (e.g., comparison to NS speech). If individuals differ in terms of their ability to do this, we can assume that their success in language learning will also differ. We point to a number of studies that have considered this relationship.

An early study examining interaction and working memory was by Mackey et al. (2002), who found a relationship among working memory capacity, noticing, and development. They investigated the acquisition of English questions by Japanese NSs. They found that there were different benefits based on working memory capacity. Individuals with lower working memory capacity showed greater gains from interaction immediately following the interaction, but those gains disappeared two weeks later on a delayed posttest. The opposite was found with higher working memory capacity individuals who showed benefits on a delayed test. These results are quite interesting in terms of what they might reveal about the relationship between learning and working memory capacity. Mackey et al. (2002, p. 204) suggest that "those with high WM [working memory] took longer to consolidate and make sense of the feedback given them, reflecting change only after an interval." Higher working memory individuals were able to assimilate more information from feedback. They were able to do just what one imagines learners can do: they recall what has been said, they compare the input with their own output, and ultimately they understand what the result of the comparison means. This takes time and was not revealed until a later posttest. Those with lower working memory capacity could make immediate modifications, but did not complete the process. In other words, the emphasis for them was on storage but not processing, whereas the emphasis for the higher group was on storage *and* processing.

Furthering the role of working memory is a study by Révész (2012) who investigated 1) working memory capacity by Hungarian learners of English and 2) the effectiveness of recasts. With regard to working memory, those with high phonological working memory scores performed better on oral tests; those who performed well on a complex working memory test (reading span, a task in which memory and processing are measured) did better on written tests. This study is intriguing on a number of fronts and points to further research in which different types of feedback are provided to learners whose working memory capacities differ based on a variety of working memory tests.

Another study considering recasts was conducted with Canadian franco-phone speakers learning English (Trofimovich et al., 2007). As with the study by Révész, different types of working memory tests were given to their thirty-two participants. The findings support the role of working memory and a learner's language analytic ability in the interpretation of recasts. They conclude with the observation that "L2 learning [involves] the development of flexible and fluent cognitive processing skills in an unpredictable, often changeable interactive environment" (p. 195).

Goo (2012) also looked at recasts, but added metalinguistic feedback to his investigation of the working memory capacity of Korean learners of English. An interesting finding was that working memory capacity affected the bene-fits of recasts but not those of metalinguistic feedback. In other words, attention, as a critical part of working memory, is important for recasts but not for metalinguistic feedback. This, of course, makes sense because meta-linguistic feedback provides specific information about an error. Recasts, on the other hand, require that the learner "work" at understanding feedback. As Goo points out, "[t]the noticing of recasts . . . necessitates cognitive control of attentional resources because it requires learners to engage in cognitive comparisons" (p. 465).

Li (2013) examined the effects of different types of feedback based on two components of aptitude: 1) language analytic ability and 2) working memory capacity. His participants were seventy-eight English learners of Chinese who received feedback on the Chinese classifier system (a noun-modifying system). There were two types of feedback provided: 1) recasts, which were referred to as implicit feedback, and 2) metalinguistic correction, referred to as explicit correction. His data showed that language analytic ability influenced the ability to reap benefit from recasts and working memory was related to the impact of explicit feedback. This differs from Goo's results and may have to do with the particular grammatical structure involved. Clearly, this is a direction for add-itional research.

Yilmaz (2013) investigated the same two constructs as those in Li (2013) (working memory and language analytic ability) to understand their effect on the benefits of recasts and explicit correction. The study involved forty-eight English speakers learning Turkish and focused on their production of locatives and plurals. Three findings are of note: 1) higher cognitive ability learners benefitted more from explicit correction than those with lower abilities; 2) explicit correction was better than recasts only for those learners with higher cognitive abilities; and 3) working memory capacity did not benefit perform-ance following a recast. (Sagarra (2007) found the opposite, but there may have been a difference in the salience of the way the feedback was provided.)

The studies reported thus far have dealt with feedback types. Mackey et al. (2010) considered a different part of interaction, namely modified output. Their investigation looked at the relationship between working memory capacity and output. Their data came from forty-two university English-speaking learners in their fourth semester of Spanish. An illustration of modified output from their study is provided in Example 4.1 originally Example 1.9, repeated here for the sake of convenience.

Example 4.1

NNS: necesita *doble a la derecha
     'you need * turn to the right'
NS: necesit . . .?
     'you need . . .?'
NNS: necesita doblar a la derecha
     'you need to turn to the right'

Their results showed a positive relationship between the production of modified output and an individual's working-memory score; learners with higher working memories produce a greater amount of modified output. Thus, greater processing capacity leads to more production.

4.2 Inhibition

We turn next to inhibition and two recent studies that investigated this construct in the context of interaction, one in an FTF interaction and the other in a CMC environment, and found opposing results. When learning a language, we are confronted with a wealth of information (e.g., syntax, morphology, phonology, semantics), often simultaneously. This can be overwhelming and often requires that we block out some stimuli to focus on others. Inhibition is the phenomenon of inhibiting certain information while attending to other. Bialystok et al. (2004) argued that the fact of being bilingual is beneficial to inhibitory control.

Gass et al. (2013) investigated the learning of noun–adjective agreement by twenty-nine English-speaking learners of Italian. The learners were involved in an interactive task in which feedback was provided. They were also given a working memory task and an inhibition task (Stroop test). Inhibitory tasks measure the ability to inhibit stimuli that are irrelevant in order to make fast and accurate decisions. The authors considered learning based on gains from a pretest to a posttest and considered those gains as they related to learner characteristics (working memory capacity and ability to inhibit). With regard to working memory scores, they did not find differential learning results. However, when considering different abilities to inhibit information, they did find differences. Specifically, those who were better able to inhibit information learned more.

A second study by Yilmaz and Sağdiç (2019) also looked at noun–adjective agreement with forty-three English-speaking learners of Spanish. They measured inhibitory control through a modified version of the Eriksen Flanker test. The interactive task in which learners had to describe to an NS of Spanish was computer mediated. There were three timing modes of feedback: one was deemed immediate (within forty seconds of an error), another was referred to as delayed, and a third group received no feedback. In the delayed group, the NS created an MS Word file in which errors were listed along with a reformulation. This was presented to each learner at the end of the task. They found no difference between the two feedback groups in relation to inhibitory control. What was interesting, however, is that learners with lower inhibitory control had higher gains in some of their tests. There are a number of differences between this study and the Gass et al. (2013) study that are in need of further exploration. For example, the materials used differed, as did, perhaps most importantly, the definition of immediate feedback. In the Gass et al. study, feedback was immediate; in the Yilmaz and Sağdiç study, it was within forty seconds.

Linck and Weiss (2011) investigated a number of individual characteristics including working memory, motivation, anxiety, and inhibitory control. Their participants were English-speaking learners of German (first semester) or Spanish (third semester). For the purposes of this section, the characteristic that predicted differences at early stages of learning was working memory, but not inhibitory control. Second, working memory (and not inhibitory control) predicted larger proficiency gains. Note that this study was not conducted within an interactive context; yet, many questions remain.

4.3 Anxiety

Anxiety has had a long history in SL research in general, often investigated within the context of a classroom. There is little research on interaction and anxiety. One study (Jeong et al., 2016) used brain imaging to determine effects of anxiety. Thirty native speakers of Japanese with English as an L2 participated in the study, which involved "simulated" conversation in which participants saw a video of an actor performing a particular action. They were to "talk" to the actor – saying something like *What kind of music are you playing?* – addressing their remarks to a video in which the actor was playing a guitar. In other instances, actors described the video, as in *He is playing the guitar now*. The first was intended to simulate a conversation (potentially anxiety-provoking) and in the second there was no communication. They found that the brain networks in the communication task were sensitive to levels of anxiety and to proficiency.

Valmori (2016) took this research a step further. Her study began with the assumption that interaction-based learning was better for some learners than for others. She pointed out that many individual variables have been investigated as a trait of an individual (e.g., working memory), but not as a variable state. She investigated in-the-moment anxiety and the impact on interaction-based learning. Her twenty-one participants were English-speaking learners of Italian who performed communicative tasks with an NS and an NNS, focusing on the acquisition of gender agreement and past tense. Following the tasks, they were shown a video of their interaction and, using MacIntyre's (2012) idiodynamic rating, rated their level of anxiety. In interviews that followed ratings, they were shown a diagram of their ratings (see Figure 4.1) and asked why they had rated anxiety in the way they did across the interaction (e.g., *Why did you feel more [or less] anxious at that point?*). The y-axis in Figure 4.1 indicates the degree of anxiety with everything above the line at 0 being high anxiety and below it being low anxiety. The x-axis represents the time duration of the interaction. Their learning was measured by fluency, accuracy, and increased number of attempts of use. Learners were categorized into three anxiety-level groups (high, medium, low). There were a number of interesting findings. First, anxiety ratings fluctuated based on task type (spot-the-difference versus

Figure 4.1 Graph of idiodynamic rating of anxiety over time

storytelling) and on interlocutor in the storytelling task (which participants stated was more challenging and anxiety-provoking). Second, there was considerable variation in the amount of anxiety across an interactive event. Third, Valmori considered the relationship among anxiety, improvement, and feedback. Across the three anxiety groups, gain scores and negotiation of meaning did not differ. This is clearly an area ripe for further research, as these results differ from previous findings (e.g., Rassaei, 2015; Sheen, 2008). It should be noted that Valmori's is the only moment-by-moment account of anxiety during interaction.

Nagle et al. (in press) took a different perspective and examined participant perceptions of anxiety and engagement in comprehension. They recognized the multifaceted nature of anxiety and engagement. For their purposes, anxiety involves "perceived stress, worry, or nervousness . . . while completing a task." Engagement is operationalized as the "perceived degree of a speaker's collaborativeness." Participants were English learners who performed three dyadic interactive tasks and did periodic ratings during the interaction of their own and their partner's levels of anxiety and collaborativeness. Their findings suggested that partner anxiety and collaborativeness predicted comprehensibility, but this was not independent of task. This study is unique in that it considers comprehensibility as a function of anxiety.

4.4 Learner Backgrounds

4.4.1 WEIRD Participants

Throughout the history of SLA research, the use of human subjects has depended on availability and convenience. This results in most studies focusing on language learning in university or other academic settings. One can see how this can lead to a bias in our findings because there are many individuals who learn language outside of a formal academic environment. Andringa and Godfroid (2020, p. 134) put it as follows: "If the selection of participants is somehow biased, then the reliability of researchers' statements about the behavior under investigation is compromised (Henrich et al., 2010). In practice, however, participant selection is almost always biased." The bias in SLA and many other social sciences comes from the fact that participants are from a limited background, namely Western, Educated, Industrialized, Rich, and Democratic (WEIRD) contexts. Plonsky (2015) has estimated that 67 percent of SLA research is based on data from WEIRD populations. But SLA is not alone; Arnett (2008), on the basis of publications in psychology journals, estimated that 80 percent of psychology data are from university students, and even more limiting is the fact that 90 percent are from North America and

Europe. Sible Andringa and Aline Godfroid have entered into an interesting project which they call *SLA-for-all Reproducibility*. In collaboration with Open Science, they are putting together a collection of studies that address this lack. That is, studies will use non-WEIRD populations as their participants. Thus, there is a major emphasis to broaden research to include non-WEIRD populations. We next turn to two areas where there has been some effort to go beyond the typical profile of participants: literacy and age.

4.4.2 Literacy

WEIRD populations are by definition composed of educated and literate individuals. Tarone and Bigelow have been influential in their insistence on going outside of WEIRD populations, long before others began to follow in this important research direction. Bigelow and Tarone have called for research with literate and/or low-literate individuals (Bigelow et al., 2006; Bigelow & Tarone, 2004; Tarone & Bigelow, 2005, 2007). They argue cogently that this understudied population is crucial if we are to understand anything more than how second languages are learned by (primarily) university-level students. We emphasize two of their studies in which they consider how L2 oral input is processed by this group (Bigelow et al., 2006; Tarone & Bigelow, 2007). First, Bigelow et al. (2006) and Bigelow (2007) focused on oral feedback to SL learners who had English reading abilities at the level of elementary school pupils, but given residence in an English-speaking country, their oral English was fluent, albeit not always grammatical. They replicated a study by Philp (2003) in which university students showed a high level of recall or uptake when presented with recasts. The participants in the Bigelow et al. and Bigelow studies were illiterate or moderately literate Somali refugees. Their behavior in response to recasts differed from that of the university students in Philp's study in that there was a significant difference between correct and incorrect recall. Thus, alphabetic print literacy is definitely related to recall of oral recasts. Second, Tarone and Bigelow (2007) furthered this research by qualitatively examining in depth one learner who exhibited very little noticing of recasts that were provided to him. They concluded that "interactional feedback in the form of recasts had very little impact on the ability of low literate learners to produce targeted linguistic segments correctly. The lower the literacy level of the learner, the less likely it was that learners would recall, either correctly or with some modification, the provided recasts" (p. 119).

4.4.3 Age

Following in the call for research beyond WEIRD participants is a study by Mackey and Sachs (2012) focusing on working memory and interaction, but on a different population than is usually investigated, namely the elderly. Their participants were L2 learners of English (Spanish as an L1) between the ages of sixty-five and eighty-nine. Their data came from a working memory task and a picture-description task in which the participants were given feedback. In Example 4.2 we provide an example of the exchange between a learner and an NS of English.

Example 4.2

Nuria (aged seventy-seven) is a Spanish speaker and Valerie is an NS of English

Nuria:	There are some . . . body, body? Somebody . . . in the, in the sand? Um, boy, boy. There are some boy in the, in the sand?
Valerie:	Is there a boy? Yes.
Nuria:	Yes. She's eh . . . He he is . . . he is doing xxxx?
Valerie:	What is he doing?
Nuria:	What he is doing, no. What, what he doing?
Valerie:	What is he doing?
Nuria:	What is he doing?
Valerie:	He's playing, in the sand.
Nuria:	Playing.

Nuria is given a range of feedback types (e.g., recasts, *What is he doing?*, confirmation checks, *Is there a boy?*). This study must be considered preliminary because of its small sample size, but it is illustrative of the learning profiles of this age group. There was some improvement, but there was not the same degree of sustained development as one finds with younger learners. Working memory did seem to play a role, however, in that those with the highest working memory capacity showed improvement on an immediate posttest, but none of the low working memory participants did. This study is important not only for the findings, which are suggestive but in need of larger-scale investigations, but also because it takes SLA research out of its "comfortable" university environment into an understudied population. The importance of expanding the population base cannot be overestimated.

4.4.4 Cognitive Creativity

Cognitive creativity is a relatively new individual difference. One important study was conducted by McDonough et al. (2015) whose participants were Thai students studying English. The students participated in a problem-solving task and took a standard test of creativity. The students were determined to be either high or low creative. Creativity was positively related to the questions the participants asked (e.g., *Anyone want to say anything else?*) and to coordination, including the use of *and* (e.g., *You guys suffer from extreme sea sicknesses* and *you guys already have minor symptoms*). Example 4.3 between two high creative students is illustrative.

Example 4.3

Science researcher:	How long can your little medicine—
Veterinarian:	Last? How long will it last? Well depends if you guys keep getting sick then it won't last long but . . . if we use it wisely you guys can survive for a long time
Science researcher:	Really?
Veterinarian:	Yeah I'll just you know keep you guys healthy because I'm a vet
Science researcher:	Vet? It's a medicine for an animals?
Veterinarian:	Well technically our bodies work pretty much identical so—
Science researcher:	Really?
Veterinarian:	So what?

These high creative students use questions for a variety of purposes. For example, the veterinarian uses a question to frame what she wants to say and then answers her own question. A question is also used to express doubt (*Really?*); it is used for clarification (*It's a medicine for an animals?*); and, in the last line, a question is used to express opposition.

Mackey (2020) describes ongoing research by Mackey et al. (2014) regarding creativity and learning that appears to be promising in our understanding of this individual characteristic. They are collecting data related to working memory and anxiety, emphasizing the need to understand not only single characteristics but also how they interact.

4.5 Conclusion

There are many individual differences that can be explored with regard to interaction. We have only touched on a few in this part of our Element. All of these are in further need of exploration as are others (e.g., grit) where there has not yet been an understanding of the individual characteristic as it relates to interaction. In Section 5, we turn to a discussion of pedagogical implications and applications of interaction.

5 What Are the Implications for Pedagogy?

The wealth of interaction research in the field of SLA has resulted in important advancements in the teaching of languages, and years of continuing classroom research in instructed SLA has strengthened our understanding of how interaction facilitates the process of acquiring an SL. In this section, we examine how the cognitive interactionist approach has affected the teaching of SLs. We consider how interaction research has contributed to changes in teaching methodologies from earlier grammar-based methods to a focus on communicative language teaching, task-based learning, and CMC. We discuss the importance of input, output, and negotiation of meaning in current SL and FL classrooms and how attempts to integrate more interaction have led to changes in materials and practices in L2 pedagogy. We also illustrate how research on corrective feedback in interaction has influenced teacher and peer feedback in the L2 classroom.

Long (2015) is clear about the relationship between teaching and theory. With specific reference to what he refers to as the *cognitive-interactionist theory of ISLA [instructed second language acquisition]*, he notes: "Of special importance is the interaction between input sensitivity and the perceptual salience of linguistic features, the hypothesized combination of learner-internal and input differences minimally required to account for the facts about variation in between-learner and within-learner achievement" (p. 60).

5.1 Implications of Interaction Research on Language Teaching Methodology

5.1.1 Communicative Language Teaching

Interaction research in SLA has played a crucial part in the swinging of the pendulum from traditional grammar translation-based teaching methodologies to more communicative language teaching methodologies that focus on genuine communication, although communicative language teaching is often used only to refer to classes taught in the target language. As the goals of language teaching have become more focused on producing functionally proficient speakers of the L2 and less focused on reading and translating written L2 texts, pedagogical methods have become more based on communication, expression of meaning, and contextualized language (Ellis, 2003; Shrum &

Glisan, 2015). In recent decades, a concern with specific methods has been replaced by a focus on learner outcomes, proficiency levels, and assessment of proficiency (Richards & Rodgers, 2014; Shrum & Glisan, 2015). This focus on proficiency can be seen in the widespread use of the levels of the ACTFL Proficiency Guidelines (e.g., Intermediate High, Advanced Low) in the placement of students on courses, the organization of programs, and the assessing of student progress (American Council on the Teaching of Foreign Languages (ACTFL), 2012).

The field of world language education reflects the importance of conversational interaction among learners, the teacher, and other speakers of the target language in the national standards, which guide the profession and are the basis of teachers' daily lesson planning. In the ACTFL World-Readiness Standards for Learning Languages (W-RSLLs), the importance of conversational interaction in the L2 is reflected in the very first standard of interpersonal communication, which states: "Learners interact and negotiate meaning in spoken, signed, or written conversations to share information, reactions, feelings, and opinions" (National Standards Collaborative Board, 2015). The primacy of interpersonal communication in the target language in today's national teaching standards indicates the foundational role of interaction in the modern language classroom.

The importance of both interaction in the communicative language classroom and interaction research is also evident in present-day expectations of new language teachers' oral and written proficiency in the target language. World language educator preparation programs now require newly licensed world language teachers to demonstrate a high degree of proficiency in the interpersonal and presentational modes of communication. In order to receive from ACTFL and the Council for the Accreditation of Educator Preparation (CAEP) the national recognition for their teacher training programs that is necessary for accreditation purposes, university language education programs must expect a high level of language proficiency from the teachers they matriculate. New language teachers are expected to achieve a level of Advanced Low on the Oral Proficiency Interview (OPI) and the Writing Proficiency Test (WPT) (or of Intermediate High in the case of languages such as Chinese, Japanese, and Arabic) (ACTFL, 2015; US Department of State, n.d.). An Advanced Low level of proficiency means that a learner of the L2 can "narrate and describe in the major time frames of past, present, and future in paragraph-length discourse with some control of aspect." It also indicates that the learner is able to "contribute to the conversation with sufficient accuracy, clarity, and precision to convey their intended message without misrepresentation or confusion" and to "be understood by native speakers unaccustomed to dealing with non-natives" (ACTFL, 2012, p. 6). In order for new teachers of languages (and here we focus on NNSs of the target language) to achieve such proficiency in the interpersonal mode of communication, their own language learning experiences will have had to contain a great deal of conversational interaction. Furthermore, new teachers need such a degree of proficiency in order to carry out interaction activities in their classrooms with their learners and be able to "speak in an unscripted, spontaneous manner and to tailor their speech so it is comprehensible to students" (Shrum & Glisan, 2015, p. 78). The ability to translate from the L1 to the L2 does not suffice for the modern language teacher whose objective is to produce functionally proficient speakers of the L2.

This focus on interpersonal communication and interacting conversationally in the L2 is also evident in the best teacher practices of the profession, such as the current expectation of 90 percent+ target language use. In 2010, ACTFL released a position statement asserting that all FL teaching should be done at least 90 percent in the target language for all levels of proficiency, from the first day of instruction. By conducting the class 90 percent in the L2, teachers are able to maximize their learners' exposure to input in the L2 and provide more opportunities for classroom interaction in the L2 (ACTFL, 2010).

The focus on interaction in communicative language teaching is obvious too in the materials that language teachers employ in the classroom. Gone are the days of discrete-point cloze tests of verb conjugations and the meaningless pronunciation drills of earlier language teaching methodologies like grammar-translation and audiolingualism. World language teaching methods courses train new teachers to engage their students with activities where the students must actually speak the target language and express meaning. New teachers are trained to use interpersonal mode of communication activities that are designed to garner greater conversational interaction and negotiation of meaning, such as picture-description tasks, info gaps, surveys, interviews, spot-the-difference tasks, jigsaws, role plays, and debates (Shrum & Glisan, 2015), all of which have figured prominently in research on interaction, highlighted in previous sections.

5.1.2 Task-Based Language Teaching (TBLT)

In addition to contributing to the movement toward a more communicative language classroom, the interactionist approach has inspired a focus on task-based language teaching (TBLT). Long (2015) is clear about this when he says that the *cognitive-interactionist theory* (p. 60) "and related empirical findings ... provide the main psycholinguistic underpinnings for TBLT" (p. 61). TBLT takes advantage of the facilitative effects of L2 interaction and refers to language teaching "based in syllabi grounded in the real-world daily tasks a specific group of learners needs to accomplish in their second language" (Mackey, 2020, p. 212). Bygate et al. (2001) suggest that TBLT has actually superseded or become a "latter day subvariant" of communicative language teaching (p. 230). When learners complete a task together in the classroom, they are communicating and negotiating meaning, they are focused on their own language use, not the teacher's, and they cooperate to attain a particular goal, each learner having particular responsibilities in the group (Shrum & Glisan, 2015).

Long is one of the earlier proponents of tasks as the basis of second language syllabi. In 2015 he made an oft-misunderstood distinction between TBLT and tblt. The former reflects tasks used in a pedagogical context based on task-based analysis to determine task needs (what he refers to as *target tasks*, p. 6) for a particular group of students. In other words, what are the real-world tasks that a particular group of students will be engaged in? Lowercase tblt refers to tasks (regardless of relevance and not based on needs analysis) that are used in a variety of syllabus types including those based on particular grammar points. Thus, a task in this context is designed to make use of a grammar point and may or may not be anything related to a real-world task that a student is likely to engage in.

A task has been defined in various ways in SLA and language education. Long (2015, p. 6) provides the following definition of a task: "[I]n TBLT [task] has its normal non-technical meaning. Tasks are the real-world activities people think of when planning, conducting, or recalling their day. That can mean things like brushing their teeth, preparing breakfast, reading a newspaper . . .." Other definitions appear as well: "a piece of classroom work which involves learners in comprehending, manipulating, producing, or interacting in the target language while their attention is principally focused on meaning rather than form" (Nunan, 1989, p. 10); "an activity in which . . . meaning is primary . . . and there is some sort of relationship to the real world" (Skehan, 1996, p. 38); and "an activity which requires learners to use language, with emphasis on meaning, to attain an objective" (Bygate et al., 2001, p. 12). Thus, there are various components that are shared (i.e., an activity), but there are others that are not shared (e.g., Long's "real-world activities," the attention on meaning and not form of Nunan and Bygate et al.) and others that are partially shared (Long's real-world and Skehan's "some sort of relationship to the real world").

Ellis (2003) stated that a task has several critical features: it must be a work plan, have a primary focus on meaning, involve real-world language processes, involve cognitive processes, and have a communicative outcome, and it can involve all four language skills. Examples of such real-world, authentic tasks in the SLA literature include reserving a theater ticket, writing out a check (Ellis, 2003), giving directions on a map, providing feedback on another learner's conference abstract (Mackey, 2020), and researching what movie to see and convincing one's group mates to see it (Wilson-Duffy, 2003). In the classroom, teachers may use the term *task* synonymously with *activity* (Bygate et al., 2001; Shrum & Glisan, 2015). Some tasks which fall into the category of more traditional in-class language activities have been used in certain studies, for instance jigsaw activities (Pica et al., 1993; Swain & Lapkin, 2001), dicto-glosses (Swain & Lapkin, 2001; Wajnryb, 1990), oral narratives (Bygate, 2001; Ortega, 2005), spot-the-difference tasks (Ellis, 2003), and information-gap activities (Pica, 2005). Swain and Lapkin (2001) pointed out that such tasks engage learners in collaboration, as well as involving them in linguistic problem-solving and the production of some spoken or written text.

Ellis (2003) differentiated between language teaching which is task-supported and that which is task-based. Task-supported language teaching refers to language teaching that may still follow the traditional present, practice, produce (Ellis, 2003; Skehan, 1996), known as the PPP approach. In the task-supported language teaching context, linguistic content is still presented by the instructor, practiced by the students, and then produced by the students, which is the stage in which the task is completed. It is difficult to ensure, however, that the intended target of linguistic practice (e.g., a particular verb form) will in fact be present in the task once the students are working on their own. In a TBLT context, the tasks that the learners carry out make up the entire curriculum of the course. There is no expectation that particular linguistic content will be used during the carrying out of the tasks. In a TBLT approach, the learners' needs for authentic L2 communication are evaluated, and tasks are designed based on those authentic learner needs (Mackey, 2020).

An important goal of SL teachers is building a collaborative discourse community of learners in the classroom (Glisan & Donato, 2017; Shrum & Glisan, 2015). TBLT sets the stage for the type of dialogic interaction in real-world, meaning-focused contexts that can facilitate acquisition. TBLT has been found to be an effective means of supporting L2 learning (Cobb, 2010; Keck et al., 2006; Mackey, 2020).

5.1.3 Computer-Mediated Communication (CMC)

Whereas much interaction research in the 1980s and 1990s focused on investigating the relationship between interaction and L2 development, interaction research has more recently branched into the area of technology (Mackey, 2020). Researchers in more recent decades have investigated how interaction facilitates language acquisition when that interaction takes place in an electronic format (Mackey & Goo, 2007; Ziegler, 2016). This focus on interaction in CMC is reflected in current FL pedagogy as well. Language teachers today use the wealth of internet resources to supply their students with target language input in the form of videos, music, films, and other authentic materials from the target language culture.

The research findings that support the role of interaction in L2 learning have led to the development of the first national content standard of FL teaching (W-RSLL 1.1), which dictates that learners of languages interact and negotiate meaning (National Standards Collaborative Board, 2015). This first standard is focused on the interpersonal mode of communication, which refers to a two-way, back-and-forth exchange of information (i.e., interaction) that is spontaneous, not scripted, meaningful, and likely contains an information gap where "one speaker seeks to acquire information that the other speaker has" (Shrum & Glisan, 2015, p. 240). This interaction and negotiation of meaning is considered the interpersonal mode of communication regardless of whether it occurs FTF or online or even via texting. Today's language teachers seek out opportunities to engage their learners in the interpersonal mode through conversations with NSs of the target language using such vehicles as Talk Abroad, WeSpeke, and Skype. Likewise, language teachers set up e-pal exchanges for their learners with NSs and use the pervasiveness of cell phones among young learners through apps such as WhatsApp and HelloChat to provide learners with the opportunity to chat on their cell phones with NSs in target language communities far away.

5.2 Input, Output, and Negotiation of Meaning in the L2 Classroom

Decades of SLA research findings confirming that L2 interaction is facilitative of acquisition have had important implications for L2 pedagogy (see also the discussion in Section 2 regarding sociocultural theory and its applications in the classroom). In the current L2 classroom, teachers seek to create environments that are rich in target language input, as well as opportunities for output, interaction, and negotiation of meaning among learners. The cognitive interactionist approach has led to important developments in the field of language teaching.

5.2.1 Input in the L2 Classroom

The crucial role in language learning of copious amounts of target language input is undisputed in the field of SL pedagogy. Certainly, one of the most significant effects that we see in the language pedagogy of Krashen's

Monitor Model is the importance of comprehensible input (1982, 1985), as discussed in Sections 1 and 3. Krashen's input hypothesis stated that L2 input must be slightly above the learner's current comprehension level (in his terms, i +1) in order for acquisition to occur. The role of comprehensible input in the target language intuitively appeals to language teachers, and methods courses for language teachers are chock full of strategies for making the target language input more comprehensible. These strategies include the heavy use of visuals, realia, gestures, facial expressions, written language on the whiteboard, drawings, repetition, and the connecting of movement with language (e.g., total physical response (TPR), Asher, 1996). Glisan and Donato (2017) recognize teachers facilitating target language comprehensibility for learners as a high leverage teaching practice, or a practice that will "promote higher gains in student learning over other teaching practices" in world language education (Hlas & Hlas, 2012, p. s76). Glisan and Donato (2017) state that teachers must make their target language classroom talk comprehensible by frequently checking comprehension, questioning learners, cueing the responses they expect from learners, and having learners show their understanding by gestures or manipulating objects and images. While we recognize the significance of the role of comprehensible input, we refer the reader to discussions in Gass et al. (2020) for a clear understanding of the theoretical limitations of this construct.

The role of input in SLA and world language education continues to be undisputed, as our understanding of this essential component has become more refined. Gass' SLA model (Gass, 1988, and discussed in Gass et al., 2020) brings in the notion of *apperception*, which Gass et al. (2020) refer to as "the process of understanding by which newly observed qualities of an object are related to past experiences. In other words, past experiences relate to the selection of what might be called *noticed* material. Apperception is an internal cognitive act, identifying a linguistic form as being related to some prior knowledge" (p. 578). Apperceived input, in this model, is converted in the learner's system into intake (Gass, 1988). In the model, the L2 input that the learner apperceives, or notices, may go through a process of negotiation between the learner and an NS (or a more proficient learner). Once there is an indication of the need for modification in the interaction episode, the NS may modify the input to make it more comprehensible to the learner. It is at this point that the apperceived input becomes comprehended input in the learner's system. The learner then employs language universals and prior linguistic knowledge of both the L1 and the L2 to assimilate that comprehended input into the learner's system, that is, to go through a process of intake.

Target language input is, of course, essential in the model for the integration of this assimilated material in the learner's system.

As acquisition of the target language depends on the provision of input in the target language, language teachers today seek to supply their students with input that is comprehensible and can be used during further interaction episodes. This target language input used by language teachers refers not just to written texts for learners to translate, as was common practice in earlier teaching methodologies, but also to authentic oral, written, and video texts from the target language culture for learners to interpret. In fact, a staple of world language instruction today is *authentic materials*. Galloway (1998, p. 133) defines authentic materials or resources as those "written and oral communications produced by members of a language and culture group for members of the same language and culture group" that ". . . invite observation of a culture talking to itself, not to outsiders." Such authentic materials are not teacher-made, simplified, pedagogical materials; rather, they are actual texts from the target language community, and therefore contain more realistic and interesting, albeit challenging, samples of language. Authentic materials used in language classes range from bus tickets and TV weather reports to literary masterpieces and popular music videos; from TV channel listings and airport announcements to newspaper editorials and poetry. The key factor is that the authentic materials are in the target language written not for language learners but for real-world communication purposes. The use of authentic materials in L2 pedagogy is thanks in large part to years of research conducted in the interactionist framework supporting the essentialness of target language input.

5.2.2 Output in the L2 Classroom

Although target language input is an essential component of language acquisition, it is not a sufficient component. The output hypothesis (Swain, 1985, 1995) states that learners of an L2 need not only to receive abundant input in the target language but also to actually produce the language in the L2, and that output forces them to move from producing the language simply in a semantic, lexically dependent fashion to producing it in a syntactically and morphologically target-like (i.e., grammatically correct) and pragmatically appropriate way. No longer is output considered simply the end-product of a language lesson, or that which learners have learned about the language from the teacher. Output, according to Swain, is a necessary component in the language acquisition process. Through comprehensible, or pushed, output, learners can notice where their production is falling short of target-like forms or where they lack knowledge of the L2. Additionally, comprehensible output gives learners the opportunity to hypothesize about specific meanings and forms in the target language and to test these hypotheses about how the language works. Further, the process of producing output gives learners the opportunity to reflect meta-linguistically on the language produced by themselves and others (Glisan & Donato, 2017; Swain, 1995).

The output hypothesis has led to changes in the way that languages are taught. As comprehensible input is an insufficient component for language learning, teachers began to design lessons that were not merely full of rich target language input but also contained activities designed to push learners to produce compre-hensible output, activities that stretched learners' ability to make themselves understood in the language they were learning. This requires that the lessons be relevant and interesting to learners and that they be meaningful and purposeful and give learners the opportunity to express themselves not only in grammat-ically accurate but also in sociolinguistically appropriate ways (Shrum & Glisan, 2015).

Similarly, Swain and Lapkin (1998) found that language is used in collabora-tive dialogues between students not only for communication but also for cognitive processes such as generating hypotheses, testing hypotheses, and applying knowledge to solve linguistic problems. In this way, language use is also a tool for learning. A focus on cooperative learning and on creating a community of learners in today's language classroom is an important compo-nent of language teacher education. This was exemplified in Section 2, Example 2.1.

5.2.3 Negotiation of Meaning in the L2 Classroom

Conversational interaction in the L2 often results in a breakdown in communi-cation in which one speaker in the conversation indicates to the other that he/she has not understood something that was said. When this breakdown in commu-nication occurs, the speakers may attempt to rectify it through negotiation of meaning. This interaction is important for language learning because it provides the learner with opportunities for negotiation of meaning through which he or she may receive not only comprehensible input but also an awareness of the inaccuracy of the utterance (Gass & Mackey, 2006, 2020; Long, 1996). The learner therefore has an opportunity to notice the difference, or the "gap" (Schmidt & Frota, 1986), between his/her utterance (i.e., the output) and the target language input that he/she is receiving. In addition, the NS of the target language (or the more proficient learner) may modify the input that he/she is providing on realizing the learner's lack of understanding. This modified input is intended to be more comprehensible, and hence more useful to the L2 learner, and may contain repetitions, definitions, examples, paraphrasing, slower and more enunciated speech, and extralinguistic features such as gestures and reliance on background knowledge.

New teachers of foreign languages who are expected to conduct their lessons 90 percent+ in the target language are trained to use these same features in their own input to their learners in order to make the language as comprehensible as possible (Glisan & Donato, 2017; Shrum & Glisan, 2015). There is similarly a focus in the language classroom on the use of the communication strategy of circumlocution, or the various ways of describing around some particular thing or idea when you don't have the language to express it in the L2. One Spanish teacher describes this to her students as the Home Depot Strategy. When one goes to a hardware store looking for a particular tool or piece of hardware, one may not know what to call the particular tool in either the L1 or the L2, so it is necessary to describe the piece to the store employee, "I don't know what it's called, but it's that little thing that you use to ..." (P. Montaldo, personal communication, August 18, 2016). Circumlocution is an important strategy used by both language teachers and students in the L2 classroom (Glisan & Donato, 2017; Shrum & Glisan, 2015).

5.3 Corrective Feedback in the L2 Classroom

A great deal of interactionist research has been conducted over the decades on the role of negative feedback provided during interaction when breakdowns in communication occur. Negotiation of meaning episodes in L2 interaction contain various forms of feedback to the speakers, as we have shown in earlier sections of this Element. This negative feedback serves an important purpose in the conversation as it indicates to the learner that there is a problem, that the learner's own production differs from the correct form, and that there is a need for conversational repair.

Likewise, in the L2 classroom, corrective feedback serves the important purpose of alerting the learner that he/she must modify the utterance to make it comprehensible to the interlocutor. Chaudron (1977) defines corrective feedback as "any reaction of the teacher which clearly transforms, disapprovingly refers to, or demands improvement of the learner's utterance" (p. 31), or similarly, a decade later, "any teacher behavior following an error that minimally attempts to inform the learner of the fact of error" (Chaudron, 1988, p. 150). Corrective feedback is essential to the learner as it indicates a problem and can lead to the production of more target-like forms. Conversational repair by the learner is possible only when there is meaningful interaction in the classroom and is evidence of the learner becoming self-regulated in the target language, as they are better able to function on their own in the language (Hall, 2007; Shrum & Glisan, 2015).

5.3.1 Teacher Corrective Feedback

Oral corrective feedback in language classrooms has a long history of research. Studies have found that corrective feedback is beneficial to language learners (see R. Ellis, 2017 and Lyster et al., 2013 for overviews and Lyster & Saito, 2010, Li, 2010 and Brown, 2016 for meta-analyses). Lyster and Ranta (1997), in their seminal study of L2 feedback, categorized these forms of feedback as explicit correction, recasts, clarification requests, metalinguisic feedback, elicitation, and repetition. Explicit correction is when the teacher says directly to the learner, "No, you should say X." Recasts (introduced in Section 1.3.2) occur when the teacher repeats a learner's utterance but replaces the erroneous part with the target-like form, such as, "S: *Why you don't like Marc? –T: Why don't you like Marc?" (Lightbown & Spada, 2013, p. 140). A clarification request (see Section 3.1) occurs when the teacher indicates a lack of understanding, for example, by saying, "Sorry, what did you say?" Metalinguistic feedback occurs when the teacher gives the learner some kind of grammatical explanation for why the form is not correct, such as "Remember to use past tense." Elicitation (see Sections 1.3.2 and 1.3.3) is when the teacher pauses or asks the student to rephrase the utterance, as in Example 5.1.

Example 5.1

S: *My father cleans the plate.
T: (Excuse me), he cleans the _____?
S: Plates?" (Lightbown & Spada, 2013, p. 141)

Repetition refers to those instances when the teacher repeats the non-target-like utterance but with rising intonation to show that there is some question as to the correctness of the utterance. When learners respond to these forms of corrective feedback, it is referred to as uptake (Lightbown & Spada, 2013; Loewen, 2003; Shrum & Glisan, 2015).

Many studies have compared the various types of corrective feedback that occur in the L2 classroom. Recasts have been found to be a particularly common form of teacher feedback. Brown's (2016) meta-analysis found that recasts accounted for 57 percent of the feedback given, whereas prompts (e.g., elicitation, repetition, metalinguistic clues) accounted for only 30 percent. Recasts have the advantage of calling the learner's attention to a problem with form without distracting from the overall focus on communication and meaning. In this sense, recasts can be unobtrusive. It is this same unobtrusiveness that can make the corrective feedback less effective; learners may not realize at all that they are being corrected and simply think that the teacher is providing back-channeling cues or repeating what was said to indicate understanding. For this reason, recasts do not always lead to learner uptake in the way that a prompt which requires some learner response will (Lyster & Ranta, 1997). Issues surrounding recasts have been discussed in recent years with differing conclusions as to their value (e.g., Goo & Mackey, 2013: Lyster & Ranta, 2013). Despite the varying views, it does appear that recasts are theoretically, if not practically, beneficial. Individual differences (discussed in Section 4) may mitigate the effectiveness in some instances.

Certainly not all feedback is correctly interpreted by the learner who is being corrected. Mackey et al. (2000) looked at learners' perceptions of negative feedback in interactional episodes as it appeared in recasts and negotiations. They found that although learners were able to correctly identify negative feedback on phonological, lexical, and semantic forms, they generally did not correctly interpret morphosyntactic feedback. Yang and Lyster (2010) compared prompts and recasts. Prompts resulted in greater learning of regular past tense English forms (i.e., the past tense -ed morpheme), whereas learners in the prompt and recast groups showed similar gains for irregular past tense forms (e.g., fly—flew).

New language teachers are trained to provide feedback to their learners in the form of their classroom discourse. Traditionally, most classroom discourse follows the pattern of Initiate–Respond–Evaluate, or IRE. Essentially, language teachers ask a learner a question in the target language (Initiate), the leaner responds (Respond), and the teacher evaluates (Evaluate) that response in the target language with a couple of words of praise or correction (e.g., "*Molto bene!*" or "*Très bien!*"). New language teachers are trained to provide more instances of Initiate–Respond–Feedback (IRF) in their classroom discourse. Here the teacher does not evaluate the correctness of the student response but, rather, elicits more language production from the student (e.g., "Really, tell me more!" or "Why do you think that?"). In IRF sequences, the feedback may push the student to a higher level of performance (Hall, 2013; Shrum & Glisan, 2015).

When feedback should be given is an undetermined question. We argued in Section 4 that an interaction can have immediate or even delayed results. The delayed results are theoretically possible if one thinks of an interaction as a starting point for change (we referred to it as a priming device). The interaction itself makes the learner aware of a problem and it may take time to figure out how to solve the problem. The issue of the timing of feedback is a slightly different one, although, with a few exceptions, there has been scant research on this topic. One notable exception is Li et al. (2016) who argue that there may be a theoretical rationale for the benefit of delayed feedback. They point to the cognitive psychology literature and argue that delayed feedback might be "preferable because it removes the need for concurrent attention to both meaning and form and because it is better able to foster the processes of retrieval and reconsolidation . . ." (p. 278). Li et al. (2016) compared immediate and delayed corrective feedback on the acquisition of English past passives (e.g., *The driver was arrested.*). The findings were not strong, but they did reveal a slight advantage for immediate feedback on one of the two measurements used to determine learning. Li et al. (2016) suggested that feedback only contributed to the explicit knowledge of the past passive. In a controlled study, Quinn (2014) (cited in Li et al. (2016)) found no effect for feedback at all and no difference between delayed and immediate feedback. Quinn and Nakata (2017) provide an overview of research on this topic.

In sum, there are many unanswered questions related to the benefit of feedback types and to the timing of benefits. Undoubtedly, over the next few years, researchers will continue to investigate these issues and teachers will continue to evaluate the benefits of feedback in their own classrooms.

A current focus in the FL classroom on the provision of peer feedback is directly traceable to the interactionist approach. The same types of indicators that learners receive in an interaction episode with an NS or a more proficient learner which alert them to a gap between their production and the target-like form can be informative to learners in the language classroom in the form of peer feedback.

5.3.2 From Focus on FormS to Focus on Form in the L2 Classroom

In earlier grammar-based teaching methodologies, language teachers had a set of particular grammatical concepts to teach their learners in a particular order; this has been referred to in the literature as Focus on FormS (Long, 1991). With the introduction of more communicative language teaching techniques, language pedagogy became much less focused on deductive grammar teaching (i.e., presentation of a grammar rule followed by decontextualized practice of said rule, an activity devoid of meaning and communicative value) (Shrum & Glisan, 2015). In communicative language teaching, the idea is that learners naturally acquire the forms as they are exposed to enough input. Adult learners, however, benefit from some direct attention being given to instruction on the L2's grammatical forms. Language teachers today are therefore instructed to provide their learners with Focus on Form (FonF). In FonF, instructors direct learners' attention to some language form while carrying out meaning-based, contextualized pedagogic activities (Loewen & Sato, 2018). Spada (1997) describes FonF, or form-focused instruction, as "pedagogical events which occur within meaning-based approaches to L2 instruction but in which a focus on language is provided in either spontaneous or predetermined ways" (p. 73).

Loewen and Sato (2018) note: "Among a variety of focus on form techniques that teachers can utilize, corrective feedback has generated a considerable amount of research" (p. 308). In fact, FonF has been found to be common in SL classrooms (Farrokhi & Gholami; 2007; Loewen, 2003; Lyster & Ranta, 1997) and beneficial to language learning (Farrokhi et al., 2008; Shrum & Glisan, 2015). FonF that occurs in response to a particular student error is referred to as reactive FonF, while FonF that is planned ahead of time by the teacher is referred to as preemptive FonF (Ellis, 2001). The teacher may intuit or plan that a particular structure will cause difficulty for learners and address that head-on before any errors occur. Example 5.2 shows how preemptive FonF works.

Example 5.2

T: Does everyone know what urban means?
T: This sentence might be hard to understand because it's passive.

Reactive FonF, however, occurs in reaction to a learner error and can be any type of negative evidence such as a recast, a metalinguistic explanation, or repetition (Farrokhi et al., 2008).

5.4 Conclusion

The interactionist approach, over the decades, has inspired a great deal of research into how the conversational interaction that occurs between learners and NSs or more proficient learners contains opportunities for negotiation of meaning and facilitates L2 acquisition. The wealth of research findings has had important pedagogical implications. The way that second and foreign languages are taught has benefitted from the interactionist approach in terms of a shift toward more communicative language teaching, with task-based and computer-mediated methodologies, a focus on functional communicative proficiency in the target language for teachers and students, teaching materials that are focused on presenting the target language authentically and nurturing L2 communication and negotiation with real-life language contexts, and advancements in the provision of corrective feedback in the classroom through focusing on language form.

References

Abbuhl, R., Mackey, A., Ziegler, N., & Amoroso, L. (2018). Interaction and learning grammar. In J. Liontas (ed.), *The TESOL Encyclopedia of English Language Teaching* (pp. 1–7). Hoboken, NJ: Wiley-Blackwell.

Alcón-Soler, E. & García Mayo, M. P. (eds.) (2009a). *International Review of Applied Linguistics in Language Teaching, 47*(3–4).

Alcón-Soler, E., & García Mayo, M. P. (2009b). Introduction. *International Review of Applied Linguistics in Language Teaching, 47*(3–4), 239–243.

Alegría de la Colina, A., & García Mayo, M. P. (2009). Oral interaction in task-based EFL learning: The use of the L1 as a cognitive tool. *International Review of Applied Linguistics in Language Teaching, 47*(3–4), 325–345.

Aljaafreh, A., & Lantolf, J. (1994). Negative feedback as regulation and second language learning in the zone of proximal development. *The Modern Language Journal, 78*, 465–483.

Allport, A. (1989). Visual attention. In M. Posner (ed.), *Foundations of Cognitive Science* (pp. 631–682). Cambridge, MA: MIT Press.

American Council on the Teaching of Foreign Languages (ACTFL). (2010, May 22). *Use of the target language in the classroom* [Position statement]. www.actfl.org/resources/guiding-principles-language-learning/use-target-language-language-learning (accessed December 4, 2020).

American Council on the Teaching of Foreign Languages (ACTFL). (2012). *ACTFL proficiency guidelines 2012.* www.actfl.org/publications/guidelines-and-manuals/actfl-proficiency-guidelines-2012 (accessed November 30, 2020).

American Council on the Teaching of Foreign Languages (ACTFL). (2015). *ACTFL/CAEP program standards for the preparation of foreign language teachers.* www.actfl.org/sites/default/files/CAEP/ACTFLCAEPStandards2013_v2015.pdf (accessed November 30, 2020).

Andringa, S., & Godfroid, A. (2020). Sampling bias and the problem of generalizability in applied linguistics. *Annual Review of Applied Linguistics, 40*, 134–142.

Arnett, J. J. (2008). The neglected 95%: Why American psychology needs to become less American. *American Psychologist, 63*(7), 602–614.

Asher, J. (1996). *Learning Another Language Through Actions* (5th ed.). Los Gatos, CA: Sky Oaks Productions.

Azkarai, A., & García Mayo, M. P. (2016). Task repetition effects on L1 use in EFL child task-based interaction. *Language Teaching Research, 21*(4), 480–495.

Azkarai, A., & Imaz Agirre, A. (2016). Negotiation of meaning strategies in child EFL mainstream and CLIL settings. *TESOL Quarterly, 50*(4), 844–870.

Azkarai, A., & Oliver, R. (2019). Negative feedback on task repetition: ESL vs. EFL child settings. *The Language Learning Journal, 47*(3), 269–280.

Baddeley, A. D. (2000). The episodic buffer: A new component of working memory? *Trends in Cognitive Sciences, 4*, 417–423.

Baddeley, A. D. (2003a). Working memory and language: An overview. *Journal of Communication Disorders, 36*, 189–208.

Baddeley, A. D. (2003b). Working memory: Looking back and looking forward. *Neuroscience, 4*, 829–839.

Baddeley, A. D., & Hitch, G. (1974). Working memory. In G. H. Bower (ed.), *The Psychology of Learning and Motivation* (pp. 47–90). New York: Academic Press.

Baralt, M. (2013). The impact of cognitive complexity on feedback efficacy during online versus face-to-face interactive tasks. *Studies in Second Language Acquisition, 35*(4), 689–725.

Baralt, M., & Gurzynski-Weiss, L. (2011). Comparing learners' state anxiety during task-based interaction in computer-mediated and face-to-face communication. *Language Teaching Research, 15*(2), 201–229.

Baralt, M., Gurzynski-Weiss, L., & Kim, Y. (2016). The effects of task complexity and classroom environment on learners' engagement with the language. In M. Sato & S. Ballinger (eds.), *Peer Interaction and Second Language Learning: Pedagogical Potential and Research Agenda* (pp. 209–239). Amsterdam: John Benjamins.

Bialystok, E., Craik, F. I., Klein, R., & Viswanathan, M. (2004). Bilingualism, aging, and cognitive control: Evidence from the Simon task. *Psychology and Aging, 19*(2), 290–303.

Bigelow, M. H. (2007). Social and cultural capital at school: The case of a Somali teenage girl. *Literacy Institute at Virginia Commonwealth University, 7*–22.

Bigelow, M., & Tarone, E. (2004). The role of literacy level in second language acquisition: Doesn't who we study determine what we know? *TESOL Quarterly, 38*(4), 689–700.

Bigelow, M., delMas, R., Hansen, K., & Tarone, E. (2006). Literacy and the processing of oral recasts in SLA. *TESOL Quarterly, 40*(4), 665–689.

Bloomfield, L. (1933). *Language.* New York: Holt, Rinehart & Winston.

Brown, D. (2016). The type and linguistic foci of oral corrective feedback in the L2 classroom: A meta-analysis. *Language Teaching Research, 20*(4), 436–458.

Bygate, M. (2001). Effects of task repetition on the structure and control of oral languages. In M. Bygate, P. Skehan, & M. Swain (eds.), *Researching Pedagogic Tasks: Second Language Learning, Teaching and Testing* (pp. 23–48). London: Longman.

Bygate, M., Skehan, P., & Swain, M. (2001). *Researching Pedagogic Tasks: Second Language Learning, Teaching, and Testing*. New York: Routledge.

Cerezo, L. (2021). Corrective feedback in computer-mediated versus face-to-face environments. In H. Nassaji & E. Kartchava (eds.), *The Cambridge Handbook of Corrective Feedback in Second Language Learning and Teaching* (pp. 494–519). Cambridge: Cambridge University Press.

Chaudron, C. (1977). A descriptive modal of discourse in the corrective treatment of learners' errors. *Language Learning, 27*, 29–46.

Chaudron, C. (1988). *Second Language Classrooms: Research on Teaching and Learning*. Cambridge University Press.

Choi, S., & Lantolf, J. (2008). Representation and embodiment of meaning in L2 communication: Motion events in the speech and gesture of advanced L2 Korean and L2 English speakers. *Studies in Second Language Acquisition, 30*, 191–224.

Chomsky, N. (1959). Review of B. F. Skinner, *Verbal Behavior. Language, 35*, 26–58.

Cobb, M. (2010). Meta-analysis of the effectiveness of task-based interaction in form-focused instruction of adult learners in foreign and second language teaching [Unpublished doctoral dissertation]. University of San Francisco.

Corder, S. P. (1967). The significance of learners' errors. *International Review of Applied Linguistics, 5*, 161–170.

Coyle, Y., & de Larios, J. R. (2020). Exploring young learners' engagement with models as a written corrective technique in EFL and CLIL settings. *System, 95*, 102374.

Coyle, Y., Guirao, J. C., & de Larios, J. R. (2018). Identifying the trajectories of young EFL learners across multi-stage writing and feedback processing tasks with model texts. *Journal of Second Language Writing, 42*, 25–43.

De la Campa, J. C., & Nassaji, H. (2009). The amount, purpose, and reasons for using L1 in L2 classrooms. *Foreign Language Annals, 42*, 742–759.

de la Fuente, M. J. (2003). Is SLA interactionist theory relevant to CALL? A study on the effects of computer-mediated interaction in L2 vocabulary acquisition. *Computer Assisted Language Learning, 16*(1), 47–81.

Donato, R. (1988). Beyond group: A psycholinguistic rationale for collective activity in second-language learning [Unpublished doctoral dissertation]. University of Delaware.

Doughty, C. (2003). Instructed SLA: Constraints, compensation, and enhancement. In C. Doughty & M. H. Long (eds.), *The Handbook of Second Language Acquisition* (pp. 256–310). Oxford: Blackwell.

Eckerth, J. (2009). Negotiated interaction in the L2 classroom. *Language Teaching, 42*(1), 109–130.

Ellis, N. C. (1998). Emergentism, connectionism and language learning. *Language Learning, 48*, 631–664.

Ellis, N. C. (2002). Frequency effects in language processing: A review with implications for theories of implicit and explicit language acquisition. *Studies in Second Language Acquisition, 24*, 143–188.

Ellis, N. C. (2006). Language acquisition as rational contingency learning. *Applied Linguistics, 27*, 1–24.

Ellis, N. C. (2008). The dynamics of second language emergence: Cycles of language use, language change, and language acquisition. *The Modern Language Journal, 41*, 232–249.

Ellis, N. C. (2017). Salience in usage-based SLA. In S. Gass, P. Spinner, & J. Behney (eds.), *Saliency in Second Language Acquisition* (pp. 39–58). New York: Routledge.

Ellis, N. C., & Wulff, S. (2020). Usage-based approaches to SLA. In B. VanPatten, G. Keating, & S. Wulff (eds.), *Theories in Second Language Acquisition: An Introduction* (3rd ed., pp. 63–82). New York: Routledge.

Ellis, R. (1984). *Classroom Second Language Development: A Study of Classroom Interaction and Language Acquisition*. Oxford: Pergamon.

Ellis, R. (1999). *Learning a Second Language through Interaction*. Amsterdam: John Benjamins.

Ellis, R. (2001). Investigating form-focused instruction. *Language Learning, 51*(1), 1–46.

Ellis, R. (2003). *Task-Based Language Learning and Teaching*. Oxford: Oxford University Press.

Ellis, R. (2017). Oral corrective feedback in L2 classrooms: What we know so far. In H. Nassaji & E. Kartchava (eds.), *Corrective Feedback in Second Language Teaching and Learning: Research, Theory, Applications, Implications* (pp. 3–18). New York: Routledge.

Ellis, R., Loewen, S., & Erlam, R. (2006). Implicit and explicit corrective feedback and the acquisition of L2 grammar. *Studies in Second Language Acquisition, 28*(2), 339–368.

Ellis, R., Tanaka, Y., & Yamazaki, A. (1994). Classroom interaction, comprehension, and the acquisition of L2 word meanings. *Language Learning, 44*(3), 449–491.

Farrokhi, F., & Gholami, J. (2007). Reactive and preemptive language related episodes and uptake in an EFL class. *Asian EFL Journal, 9(2)*, 58–92.

Farrokhi, F., Ansarin, A. A., & Mohammadnia, Z. (2008). Preemptive Focus on Form: Teachers' practices across proficiencies. *Linguistics Journal, 3(2)*, 7–30.

Ferguson, C. (1971). Absence of copula and the notion of simplicity: A study of normal speech, baby talk, foreigner talk and pidgins. In D. Hymes (ed.), *Pidginization and Creolization of Languages* (pp. 141–150). Cambridge: Cambridge University Press.

Foster, P. (1998). A classroom perspective on the negotiation of meaning. *Applied Linguistics, 19(1)*, 1–23.

Frawley, W., & Lantolf, J. P. (1985). L2 discourse: A Vygotskian perspective. *Applied Linguistics, 6*, 19–44.

Fries, C. (1957). Foreword. In R. Lado, *Linguistics across Cultures*. Ann Arbor: University of Michigan Press.

Gallaway, C., & Richards, B. (eds.) (1994). *Input and Interaction in Language Acquisition*. Cambridge: Cambridge University Press.

Galloway, V. (1998). Constructing cultural realities: "Facts" and frameworks of association. In J. Harper, M. Lively, & M. Williams (eds.), *The Coming of Age of the Profession* (pp. 129–140). Boston: Heinle & Heinle.

Gánem Gutiérrez, A. (2008). Microgenesis, method and object: A study of collaborative activity in a Spanish as foreign language classroom. *Applied Linguistics, 29(1)*, 120–148.

García Mayo, M. P. (2002). Interaction in advanced EFL pedagogy: A comparison of form-focused activities. *International Journal of Educational Research, 37(3–4)*, 323–341.

García Mayo, M. P., & Alcón Soler, E. (2013). Negotiated input and output/interaction. In J. Herschensohn & M. Young Scholten (eds.), *The Cambridge Handbook of Second Language Acquisition* (pp. 209–229). Cambridge: Cambridge University Press.

García Mayo, M. P., & García Lecumberri, M. L. (2003). *Age and the Acquisition of English as a Foreign Language*. Clevedon, UK: Multilingual Matters.

García Mayo, M. P., & Imaz Agirre, A. (2016). Task repetition and its impact on EFL children's negotiation of meaning strategies and pair dynamics: An exploratory study. *The Language Learning Journal, 44(4)*, 451–466.

García Mayo, M. P., & Lázaro Ibarrola, A. (2015). Do children negotiate for meaning in task-based interaction? Evidence from CLIL and EFL settings. *System, 54*, 40–54.

Gass, S. (1988). Integrating research areas: A framework for second language studies. *Applied Linguistics, 9(2)*, 198–217.

Gass, S. (1997). *Input, Interaction, and the Second Language Learner.* Mahwah, NJ: Lawrence Erlbaum Associates.

Gass, S. (2010). Interactionist perspectives on second language acquisition. In R. Kaplan (ed.), *The Oxford Handbook of Applied Linguistics* (2nd ed., pp. 217–231). Oxford: Oxford University Press.

Gass, S. (2018). *Input, Interaction, and the Second Language Learner.* New York: Routledge.

Gass, S., & Mackey, A. (2006). Input, interaction and output: An overview. In K. Bardovi Harlig and Z. Dörnyei (eds.), *AILA Review* (pp. 3–17). Amsterdam: John Benjamins.

Gass, S., & Mackey, A. (2020). Input, interaction, and output in L2 acquisition. In B. VanPatten, G. Keating, & S. Wulff (eds.), *Theories of Second Language Acquisition: An Introduction* (3rd ed., pp. 192–222). New York: Routledge.

Gass, S., & Selinker, L. (1994). *Second Language Acquisition: An Introductory Course.* Hillsdale, NJ: Lawrence Erlbaum Associates.

Gass, S., & Varonis, E. (1984). The effect of familiarity on the comprehensibility of non-native speech. *Language Learning, 34*(1), 65–89.

Gass, S., & Varonis, E. (1985). Variation in native speaker speech modification to nonnative speakers. *Studies in Second Language Acquisition, 7,* 37–57.

Gass, S., & Varonis, E. (1989). Incorporated repairs in NNS discourse. In M. Eisenstein (ed.), *Variation and Second Language Acquisition* (pp. 71–86). New York: Plenum Press.

Gass, S., & Varonis, E. (1994). Input, interaction and second language production. *Studies in Second Language Acquisition, 16,* 283–302.

Gass, S., Behney, J., & Plonsky, L. (2020). *Second Language Acquisition: An Introductory Course* (5th ed.). New York: Routledge.

Gass, S., Behney, J., & Uzum, B. (2013). Inhibitory control, working memory, and L2 interaction gains. In K. Dróżdział-Szelest & M. Pawlak (eds.), *Psycholinguistic and Sociolinguistic Perspectives on Second Language Learning and Teaching: Studies in Honor of Waldemar Marton* (pp. 91–114). Berlin: Springer Verlag.

Gass, S., Mackey, A., & Ross-Feldman, L. (2005). Task-based interactions in classroom and laboratory settings. *Language Learning, 55,* 575–611.

Gass, S., Mackey, A., & Ross-Feldman, L. (2011). Task-based interactions in classroom and laboratory settings. *Language Learning (reprint), 61,* 189–220.

Gilabert, R., Barón, J. & Llanes, À. (2009). Manipulating cognitive complexity across task types and its impact on learners' interaction during oral performance. *International Review of Applied Linguistics in Language Teaching, 47*(3–4), 367–395.

Glisan, E. W., & Donato, R. (2017). *Enacting the Work of Language Instruction: High-Leverage Teaching Practices*. Alexandria, VA: American Council on the Teaching of Foreign Languages.

Goo, J. (2012). Corrective feedback and working memory capacity in interaction-driven L2 learning. *Studies in Second Language Acquisition, 34*, 445–474.

Goo, J., & Mackey, A. (2013). The case against the case against recasts. *Studies in Second Language Acquisition, 35*, 127–165.

Gurzynski-Weiss, L., & Baralt, M. (2014). Exploring learner perception and use of task-based interactional feedback in face-to-face and computer-mediated modes. *Studies in Second Language Acquisition, 36*, 1–37.

Hall, J. K. (2007). Redressing the roles of correction and repair in research on second and foreign language learning. *The Modern Language Journal, 91* (4), 511–526.

Hall, J. K. (2013). *Teaching and Researching: Language and Culture* (2nd ed.). New York: Routledge.

Hatch, E. (1978a). Acquisition of syntax in a second language. In J. C. Richards (ed.), *Understanding Second and Foreign Language Learning: Issues and Approaches* (pp. 34–69). Rowley, MA: Newbury House.

Hatch, E. (1978b). Discourse analysis and second language acquisition. In E. Hatch (ed.), *Second Language Acquisition: A Book of Readings* (pp. 401–435). Rowley, MA: Newbury House.

Hatch, E. (1983). *Psycholinguistics: A Second Language Perspective*. Rowley, MA: Newbury House.

Henrich, J., Heine, S. J., & Norenzayan, A. (2010). The weirdest people in the world? *Behavioral and Brain Sciences, 33*(2–3), 61–83.

Hlas, A. C., & Hlas, C. S. (2012). A review of high-leverage teaching practices: Making connections between mathematics and foreign languages. *Foreign Language Annals, 45*(s1), s76–s97.

Hulstijn, J., Young, R., Ortega, L., & Bigelow, M. (2014). Bridging the gap: Cognitive and social approaches to research in second language learning and teaching. *Studies in Second Language Acquisition, 36*, 361–421.

Jeong, H., Sugiura, M., Suzuki, W., Sassa, Y., Hashizume, H., & Kawashima, R. (2016). Neural correlates of second-language communication and the effect of language anxiety. *Neuropsychologia, 84*, e2–e12.

Keck, C. M., Iberri-Shea, G., Tracy-Ventura, N., & Wa-Mbaleka, S. (2006). Investigating the empirical link between task-based interaction and acquisition: A meta-analysis. In J. M. Norris & L. Ortega (eds.), *Synthesizing*

Research on Language Learning and Teaching (pp. 91–131). Amsterdam: John Benjamins.

Krashen, S. (1977). Some issues relating to the monitor model. In H. Brown, C. Yorio, & R. Crymes (eds.), *On TESOL '77: Teaching and Learning English as a Second Language: Trends in Research and Practice* (pp. 144–158). Washington, DC: Teachers of English to Speakers of Other Languages.

Krashen, S. (1982). *Principles and Practice in Second Language Acquisition*. London: Pergamon.

Krashen, S. (1985). *The Input Hypothesis: Issues and Implications*. New York: Longman.

Lado, R. (1957). *Linguistics across Cultures*. Ann Arbor: University of Michigan Press.

Lantolf, J. (2012). Sociocultural theory: A dialectical approach to L2 research. In S. Gass & A. Mackey (eds.), *The Routledge Handbook of Second Language Acquisition* (pp. 57–72). New York: Routledge.

Lantolf, J. P. (2014). The sociocultural perspective. *Studies in Second Language Acquisition*, *36*, 368–374.

Lantolf, J. P., & Thorne, S. (2006). *Sociocultural Theory and the Genesis of Second Language Development*. Oxford: Oxford University Press.

Lantolf, J. P., & Thorne, S. (2007). Sociocultural theory and second language learning. In B. VanPatten & J. Williams (eds.), *Theories in Second Language Acquisition: An Introduction* (pp. 201–224). Mahwah, NJ: Lawrence Erlbaum Associates.

Lantolf, J., Kurtz, L., & Kisselev, O. (2016). Understanding the revolutionary character of L2 development in the ZPD: Why levels of mediation matter. *Language and Sociocultural Theory*, *3*, 153–171.

Lantolf, J., Thorne, S., & Poehner, M. (2020). Sociocultural theory and second language development. In B. VanPatten, G. Keating, & S. Wulff (eds.), *Theories of Second Language Acquisition: An Introduction* (3rd ed.). New York: Routledge.

Levine, G. (2013). The case for a multilingual approach to language classroom communication. *Language and Linguistics Compass*, *7*(8), 423–436.

Li, S. (2010). The effectiveness of corrective feedback in SLA: A meta-analysis. *Language Learning*, *60*(2), 309–365.

Li, S. (2013). The interactions between the effects of implicit and explicit feedback and individual differences in language analytic ability and working memory. *The Modern Language Journal*, *97*(3), 634–654.

Li, S., Zhu, Y., & Ellis, R. (2016). The effects of the timing of corrective feedback on the acquisition of a new linguistic structure. *The Modern Language Journal*, *100*, 276–295.

Liebscher, G., & Dailey-O'Cain, J. (2009). Student and teacher use of the first language in foreign language classroom interaction: Functions and applications. In M. Turnbull & J. Dailey-O'Cain (eds.), *First Language Use in Second and Foreign Language Learning* (pp. 131–144). Clevedon, UK: Multilingual Matters.

Lightbown, P. M., & Spada, N. (2013). *How Languages Are Learned* (4th ed.). Oxford: Oxford University Press.

Linck, J. A., & Weiss, D. J. (2011). Working memory predicts the acquisition of explicit L2 knowledge. In C. Sanz (ed.), *Implicit and Explicit Language Learning: Conditions, Processes, and Knowledge in SLA and Bilingualism* (pp. 101–113). Washington, DC: Georgetown University Press.

Linck, J. A., Osthus, P., Koeth, J. T., & Bunting, M. F. (2014). Working memory and second language comprehension and production: A meta-analysis. *Psychonomic Bulletin & Review, 21,* 861–883.

Loewen, S. (2002). The occurrence and effectiveness of incidental focus on form in meaning-focused ESL lessons [Unpublished doctoral dissertation]. University of Auckland.

Loewen, S. (2003). Variation in the frequency and characteristics of incidental focus on form. *Language Teaching Research, 7,* 315–345.

Loewen, S., & Gass, S. (2021). Laboratory-based oral corrective feedback. In H. Nassaji & E. Kartchava (eds.), *The Cambridge Handbook of Corrective Feedback in Second Language Learning and Teaching* (pp. 130–146). Cambridge: Cambridge University Press.

Loewen, S., & Sato, M. (2018). Interaction and instructed second language acquisition. *Language Teaching, 51,* 285–329.

Long, M. H. (1980). Input, interaction and second language acquisition [Unpublished doctoral dissertation]. University of California.

Long, M. H. (1981). Input, interaction and second language acquisition. In H. Winitz (ed.), *Native Language and Foreign Language Acquisition: Annals of the New York Academy of Sciences Vol. 379* (pp. 259–278). New York: New York Academy of Sciences.

Long, M. H. (1983a). Native speaker/non-native speaker conversation and the negotiation of comprehensible input. *Applied Linguistics, 4*(2), 126–141.

Long, M. H. (1983b). Linguistic and conversational adjustments. *Studies in Second Language Acquisition, 5*(2), 177–193.

Long, M. H. (1983c). Native speaker/non-native speaker conversation in the second language classroom. In M. Clarke & J. Handscombe (eds.), *On TESOL '82: Pacific Perspectives on Language Learning and Teaching* (pp. 207–225). Washington, DC: TESOL.

Long, M. H. (1991). Focus on form: A design feature in language teaching methodology. In K. de Bot, R. Ginsberg, & C. Kramsch (eds.), *Foreign Language Research in Cross-Cultural Perspective* (pp. 39–52). Amsterdam: John Benjamins.

Long, M. H. (1992, March). *Input, focus on form, and second language acquisition*. Paper presented at the American Association of Applied Linguistics annual meeting, Seattle, WA.

Long, M. H. (1996). The role of the linguistic environment in second language acquisition. In W. C. Ritchie & T. K. Bhatia (eds.), *Handbook of Language Acquisition. Vol. 2: Second Language Acquisition* (pp. 413–468). New York: Academic Press.

Long, M. H. (2015). *Second Language Acquisition and Task-Based Language Teaching*. Malden, MA: Wiley Blackwell.

Lyster, R. (2019). Roles for corrective feedback in second language instruction. In C. Chapelle (ed.), *The Encyclopedia of Applied Linguistics*. Malden, MA: Wiley-Blackwell.

Lyster, R., & Ranta, L. (1997). Corrective feedback and learner uptake: Negotiation of form in communicative classrooms. *Studies in Second Language Acquisition, 19*, 36–37.

Lyster, R., & Ranta, L. (2013). Counterpoint piece: The case for variety in corrective feedback research. *Studies in Second Language Acquisition, 35*(1), 167–184.

Lyster, R., & Saito, K. (2010). Oral feedback in classroom SLA: A meta-analysis. *Studies in Second Language Acquisition, 32*(2), 265–302.

Lyster, R., Saito, K., & Sato, M. (2013). Oral corrective feedback in second language classrooms. *Language Teaching, 46*(1), 1–40.

Macaro, E. (2001). Analysing student teachers' codeswitching in foreign language classrooms: Theories and decision making. *The Modern Language Journal, 85*(4), 531–548.

MacIntyre, P. D. (2012). The idiodynamic method: A closer look at the dynamics of communication traits. *Communication Research Reports, 29*(4), 361–367.

Mackey, A. (1999). Input, interaction and second language development. *Studies in Second Language Acquisition, 21*, 557–587.

Mackey, A. (2002). Beyond production: Learners' perceptions about interactional processes. *International Journal of Educational Research, 37*, 379–394.

Mackey, A. (ed.) (2007). *Conversational Interaction in Second Language Acquisition*. Oxford: Oxford University Press.

Mackey, A. (2012). *Input, Interaction, and Corrective Feedback in L2 Learning*. Oxford: Oxford University Press.

Mackey, A. (2020). *Interaction, Feedback and Task Research in Second Language Learning: Methods and Design*. Cambridge: Cambridge University Press.

Mackey, A., & Goo, J. (2007). Interaction research in SLA: A meta-analysis and research synthesis. In A. Mackey (ed.), *Conversational Interaction in Second Language Acquisition: A Series of Empirical Studies* (pp. 407–452). Oxford: Oxford University Press.

Mackey, A., & Oliver, R. (2002). Interactional feedback and children's L2 development. *System, 30*, 459–477.

Mackey, A., & Philp, J. (1998). Conversational interaction and second language development: Recasts, responses, and red herrings? *The Modern Language Journal, 82*, 338–356.

Mackey, A., & Sachs, R. (2012). Older learners in SLA research: A first look at working memory, feedback, and L2 development. *Language Learning, 62*, 704–740.

Mackey, A., & Silver, R. E. (2005). Interactional tasks and English L2 learning by immigrant children in Singapore. *System, 33*, 239–260.

Mackey, A., Abbuhl, R., & Gass, S. (2012). Interactionist approach. In S. Gass & A. Mackey (eds.), *The Routledge Handbook of Second Language Acquisition* (pp. 7–23). New York: Routledge.

Mackey, A., Adams, R., Stafford, C., & Winke, P. (2010). Exploring the relationship between modified output and working memory capacity. *Language Learning, 60*, 501–533.

Mackey, A., Gass, S. M., & McDonough, K. (2000). How do learners perceive interactional feedback? *Studies in Second Language Acquisition, 22*, 471–497.

Mackey, A., Oliver, R., & Leeman, J. (2003). Interactional input and the incorporation of feedback: An exploration of NS-NNS and NNS-NNS adult and child dyads. *Language Learning, 53*, 35–66.

Mackey, A., Park, H., Akiyama, Y., & Pipes, A. (2014, March). The role of cognitive creativity in L2 learning processes. Paper presented at the Georgetown University Round Table, Washington, DC.

Mackey, A., Philp, J., Egi, T., Fujii, A., & Tatsumi, T. (2002). Individual differences in working memory, noticing of interactional feedback, and L2 development. In P. Robinson (ed.), *Individual Differences and Instructed Language Learning* (pp. 181–209). Philadelphia: John Benjamins.

McDonough, K., & Mackey, A. (2006). Responses to recasts: Repetitions, primed production, and linguistic development. *Language Learning, 56*, 693–720.

McDonough, K., Crawford, W., & Mackey, A. (2015). Creativity and EFL students' language use during a group problem-solving task. *TESOL Quarterly, 49*(1), 188–198.

McLaughlin, B. (1987). *Theories of Second Language Learning*. London: Edward Arnold.

Miyake, A., & Shah, P. (eds.) (1999). *Models of Working Memory: Mechanisms of Active Maintenance and Executive Control*. Cambridge: Cambridge University Press.

Muñoz, C. (ed.) (2006). *Age and the Rate of Foreign Language Learning*. Clevedon, UK: Multilingual Matters.

Nagle, C., Trofimovich, P., O'Brien, M., & Kennedy, S. (in press). Beyond linguistic features: Exploring behavioral and affective correlates of comprehensible second language speech. *Studies in Second Language Acquisition*. Published online March 23, 2021, https://lib.dr.iastate.edu/cgi/viewcontent.cgi?article=1241&context=language_pubs (accessed July 10, 2021).

Nakatsukasa, K., & Loewen, S. (2017). Non-verbal feedback. In H. Nassaji & E. Kartchava (eds.), *Corrective Feedback in Second Language Teaching and Learning: Research, Theory, Applications, Implications* (pp. 158–173). New York: Routledge.

Nassaji, H., & Kartchava, E. (eds.) (2017). *Corrective Feedback in Second Language Teaching and Learning: Research, Theory, Applications, Implications*. New York: Routledge.

Nassaji, H., & Kartchava, E. (eds.) (2021). *The Cambridge Handbook of Corrective Feedback in Second Language Learning and Teaching*. Cambridge: Cambridge University Press.

National Standards Collaborative Board (2015). *World-Readiness Standards for Learning Languages* (4th ed.). Alexandria, VA: Author.

Nunan, D. (1989). *Designing Tasks for the Communicative Classroom*. Cambridge: Cambridge University Press.

Oliver, R. (1995). Negative feedback in child NS-NNS conversation. *Studies in Second Language Acquisition*, *17*, 459–481.

Oliver, R. (1998). Negotiation of meaning in child interactions. *The Modern Language Journal*, *82*(3), 372–386.

Oliver, R. (2000). Age differences in negotiation and feedback in classroom and pairwork. *Language Learning*, *50*(1), 119–151.

Oliver, R. (2002). The patterns of negotiation for meaning in child interactions. *The Modern Language Journal*, *86*(1), 97–111.

Oliver, R. (2009). How young is too young? Investigating negotiation of meaning and corrective feedback in children aged five to seven years. In A. Mackey & C. Polio (eds.), *Multiple Perspectives on Interaction: Second Language Interaction Research in Honor of Susan M. Gass* (pp. 135–156). London: Routledge.

Oliver, R., & Azkarai, A. (2017). Review of child second language acquisition (SLA): Examining theories and research. *Annual Review of Applied Linguistics*, *37*, 62–76.

Oliver, R., & Mackey, A. (2003). Interactional context and feedback in child ESL classrooms. *The Modern Language Journal*, *87*, 519–533.

Ortega, L. (1997). Processes and outcomes in networked classroom interaction: Defining the research agenda for L2 computer-assisted classroom discussion. *Language Learning & Technology*, *1*(1), 82–93.

Ortega, L. (2005). What do learners plan?: Learner-driven attention to form during pre-task planning. In R. Ellis (ed.), *Planning and Task Performance in a Second Language* (pp. 77–109). Amsterdam: John Benjamins.

Paradis, J. (2007). Second language acquisition in childhood. In E. Hoff & M. Shatz (eds.), *Blackwell Handbook of Language Development* (pp. 387–406). Malden, MA: Blackwell.

Philp, J. (2003). Constraints on noticing the gap: Nonnative speakers' noticing of recasts in NS-NNS interaction. *Studies in Second Language Acquisition*, *25*, 99–126.

Philp, J., & Tognini, R. (2009). Language acquisition in foreign language contexts and the differential benefits of interaction. *International Review of Applied Linguistics in Language Teaching*, *47*(3–4), 245–266.

Philp, J., Adams, R., & Iwashita, N. (2013). *Peer Interaction and Second Language Learning*. New York: Routledge.

Philp, J., Oliver, R., & Mackey, A. (eds.) (2008). *Second Language Acquisition and the Younger Learner: Child's Play?* Amsterdam: John Benjamins.

Pica, T. (1987). Second language acquisition, social interaction, and the classroom. *Applied Linguistics*, *8*, 3–21.

Pica, T. (1988). Interlanguage adjustments as an outcome of NS–NNS negotiated interaction. *Language Learning*, *38*, 45–73.

Pica, T. (1994). Research on negotiation: What does it reveal about second-language learning conditions, processes, and outcomes? *Language Learning*, *44*, 493–527.

Pica, T. (1996). Second language learning through interaction: Multiple perspectives. *Working Papers in Educational Linguistics*, *12*(1), 1–21.

Pica, T. (2005). Classroom learning, teaching, and research: A task-based perspective. *The Modern Language Journal*, *89*(3), 339–352.

Pica, T., Kanagy, R., & Falodun, J. (1993). Choosing and using communication tasks for second language instruction. In G. Crookes & S. M. Gass (eds.), *Tasks and Language Learning* (pp. 9–34). Clevedon, UK: Multilingual Matters.

Pienemann, M., & Johnston, M. (1987). Factors influencing the development of language proficiency. In D. Nunan (ed.), *Applying Second Language*

Acquisition Research (pp. 45–141). Adelaide: National Curriculum Resource Centre, AMEP.

Pienemann, M., & Mackey, A. (1993). An empirical study of children's ESL development. In P. McKay (ed.), *ESL Development: Language and Literacy in Schools. Vol. 2: Documents on Bandscale Development and Language Acquisition* (pp. 115–259). Canberra: National Languages & Literacy Institute of Australia and Commonwealth of Australia.

Pienemann, M., Johnston, M., & Brindley, G. (1988). Constructing an acquisition-based procedure for second language assessment. *Studies in Second Language Acquisition, 10*, 217–243.

Pinter, A. (2006). Verbal evidence of task related strategies: Child versus adult interactions. *System, 34*, 615–630.

Plonsky, L. (2015, October). *Demographics in SLA: A systematic review of sampling practices in L2 research*. Paper presented at the Second Language Research Forum (SLRF), Atlanta, GA.

Plonsky, L., & Brown, D. (2015). Domain definition and search techniques in meta-analyses of L2 research (or why 18 meta-analyses of feedback have different results). *Second Language Research, 31*, 267–278.

Plonsky, L., & Gass, S. (2011). Quantitative research methods, study quality, and outcomes: The case of interaction research. *Language Learning, 61*, 325–366.

Polio, C., & Duff, P. (1994). Teachers' language use in university foreign language classrooms: A qualitative analysis of English and target language alternation. *The Modern Language Journal, 78*(3), 313–326.

Quinn, P. (2014). Delayed versus immediate corrective feedback on orally produced passive errors in English [Unpublished doctoral dissertation]. University of Toronto.

Quinn, P. G., & Nakata, T. (2017). The timing of oral corrective feedback. In H. Nassaji & E. Kartchava (eds.), *Corrective Feedback in Second Language Teaching and Learning: Research, Theory, Applications, Implications* (pp. 35–47). New York: Routledge.

Rassaei, E. (2015). Oral corrective feedback, foreign language anxiety, and L2 development. *System, 49*, 98–109.

Révész, A. (2012). Working memory and the observed effectiveness of recasts on different L2 outcome measures. *Language Learning, 62*(1), 93–132.

Richards, J. C., & Rodgers, T. S. (2014). *Approaches and Methods in Language Teaching*. New York: Cambridge University Press.

Robinson, P., Mackey, A., Gass, S., & Schmidt, R. (2012). Attention and awareness in second language acquisition. In S. Gass & A. Mackey (eds.), *The Routledge Handbook of Second Language Acquisition* (pp. 247–267). New York: Routledge.

Rudd, L. C., & Lambert, M. C. (2011). Interaction theory language development. In S. Goldstein & J. A. Naglieri (eds.), *Encyclopedia of Child Behavior and Development*. Boston, MA: Springer.

Russell, J., & Spada, N. (2006). The effectiveness of corrective feedback for the acquisition of L2 grammar: A meta-analysis of the research. In J. Norris & L. Ortega (eds.), *Synthesizing Research on Language Learning and Teaching* (pp. 133–163). Philadelphia: John Benjamins.

Sagarra, N. (2007). From CALL to face-to-face interaction: The effect of computer delivered recast and working memory on L2 development. In A. Mackey (ed.), *Conversational Interaction in Second Language Acquisition* (pp. 229–248). Oxford: Oxford University Press.

Saito, K., & Akiyama, Y. (2017). Video-based interaction, negotiation for comprehensibility, and second language speech learning: A longitudinal study. *Language Learning, 67*(1), 43–74.

Sato, C. (1986) Conversation and interlanguage development: Rethinking the connection. In R. Day (ed.), *Talking to Learn: Conversation in Second Language Acquisition* (pp. 23–45). Rowley, MA: Newbury House.

Saxton, M. (1997). The contrast theory of negative input. *Journal of Child Language, 24*, 139–161.

Schmidt, R. (1990). The role of consciousness in second language learning. *Applied Linguistics, 11*, 129–158.

Schmidt, R. (1993a). Awareness and second language acquisition. *Annual Review of Applied Linguistics, 13*, 206–226.

Schmidt, R. (1993b). Consciousness, learning and interlanguage pragmatics. In G. Kasper & S. Blum-Kulka (eds.), *Interlanguage Pragmatics* (pp. 21–42). New York: Oxford University Press.

Schmidt, R. (1994). Implicit learning and the cognitive unconscious: Of artificial grammars and SLA. In N. Ellis (ed.), *Implicit and Explicit Learning of Languages* (pp. 165–209). London: Academic Press.

Schmidt, R. (1995). Consciousness and foreign language learning: A tutorial on the role of attention and awareness in learning. In R. Schmidt (ed.), *Attention and Awareness in Foreign Language Learning* (Tech. Rep. No. 9, pp. 1–64). Honolulu: University of Hawai'i at Manoa, Second Language Teaching and Curriculum Center.

Schmidt, R. (2001). Attention. In P. Robinson (ed.), *Cognition and Second Language Instruction* (pp. 3–32). Cambridge: Cambridge University Press.

Schmidt, R., & Frota, S. (1986). Developing basic conversational ability in a second language: A case study of an adult learner of Portuguese. In R. Day (ed.), *Talking to Learn: Conversation in Second Language Acquisition* (pp. 237–326). Rowley, MA: Newbury House.

Sheen, Y. (2004). Corrective feedback and learner uptake in communicative classrooms across instructional settings. *Language Teaching Research, 8*(3), 263–300.

Sheen, Y. (2008). Recasts, language anxiety, modified output, and L2 learning. *Language Learning, 58*(4), 835–874.

Sheen, Y. (2010). Introduction: The role of oral and written corrective feedback in SLA. *Studies in Second Language Acquisition, 32*(2), 159–179.

Sheen, Y., & Ellis, R. (2011). Corrective feedback in language teaching. In E. Hinkel (ed.), *Handbook of Research in Second Language Teaching and Learning* (2nd ed., pp. 593–610). New York: Routledge.

Shi, G. (2004). Teacher's corrective feedback and learner repair in secondary EFL classrooms. *Foreign Language and Literature, 86*(4), 242–248.

Shrum, J., & Glisan, E. (2015). *Teacher's Handbook: Contextualized Language Instruction* (5th ed.). Boston, MA: Heinle & Heinle.

Skehan, P. (1996). A framework for the implementation of task-based instruction. *Applied Linguistics, 17*(1), 38–62.

Slabakova, R., Leal, T., Dudley, A., & Stack, M. (2020). *Generative Second Language Acquisition* (Cambridge Element). Cambridge: Cambridge University Press.

Spada, N. (1997). Form-focussed instruction and second language acquisition: A review of classroom and laboratory research. *Language Teaching, 30*(2), 73–87.

Spada, N., & Lightbown, P. (1993). Instruction and the development of questions in L2 classrooms. *Studies in Second Language Acquisition, 15*, 205–224.

Stevick, E. W. (1976). *Memory, Meaning and Method*. Rowley, MA: Newbury House.

Storch, N. (2017). Sociocultural theory in the L2 classroom. In S. Loewen & M. Sato (eds.), *The Routledge Handbook of Instructed Second Language Acquisition* (pp. 70–83). New York: Routledge.

Swain, M. (1985). Communicative competence: Some roles of comprehensible input and comprehensible output in its development. In S. Gass & C. Madden (eds.), *Input in Second Language Acquisition* (pp. 235–253). Rowley, MA: Newbury House.

Swain, M. (1993). The output hypothesis: Just speaking and writing aren't enough. *The Canadian Modern Language Review, 50*, 158–164.

Swain, M. (1995). Three functions of output in second language learning. In G. Cook & B. Seidlhofer (eds.), *Principle and Practice in Applied Linguistics* (pp. 125–144). Oxford: Oxford University Press.

Swain, M. (2000). The output hypothesis and beyond: Mediating acquisition through collaborative dialogue. In J. P. Lantolf (ed.), *Sociocultural Theory and Second Language Learning* (pp. 97–114). Oxford: Oxford University Press.

Swain, M. (2005). The output hypothesis: Theory and research. In E. Hinkel (ed.), *Handbook of Research in Second Language Teaching and Learning* (pp. 471–483). Mahwah, NJ: Lawrence Erlbaum Associates.

Swain, M. (2006). Languaging, agency, and collaboration in advanced language proficiency. In H Byrnes (ed.), *Advanced Language Learning: The Contribution of Halliday and Vygotsky* (pp. 95–108). London: Continuum.

Swain, M., & Lapkin, S. (1995). Problems in output and the cognitive processes they generate: A step towards second language learning. *Applied Linguistics*, *16*, 371–391.

Swain, M., & Lapkin, S. (1998). Interaction and second language learning: Two adolescent French immersion students working together. *The Modern Language Journal*, *82*(3), 320–337.

Swain, M., & Lapkin, S. (2001). Focus on form through collaborative dialogue: Exploring task effects. In M. Bygate, P. Skehan, & M. Swain (eds.), *Researching Pedagogic Tasks: Second Language Learning, Teaching and Testing* (pp. 99–118). London: Longman.

Swain, M., & Watanabe, Y. (2013). Languaging: Collaborative dialogue as a source of second language learning. In C. Chapelle (ed.), *The Encyclopedia of Applied Linguistics* (pp. 1–8). Hoboken, NJ: Blackwell.

Tarone, E., & Bigelow, M. H. (2005). Impact of literacy on oral language processing: Implications for second language acquisition research. *Annual Review of Applied Linguistics*, *25*, 77–97.

Tarone, E., & Bigelow, M. H. (2007). Alphabetic print literacy and processing of oral corrective feedback in the L2. In A. Mackey (ed.), *Interaction and Second Language Acquisition* (pp. 101–121). Oxford: Oxford University Press.

Thompson, G. L., & Harrison, K. (2014). Language use in the foreign language classroom. *Foreign Language Annals*, *47*(2), 321–337.

Tognini, R. (2008). Interaction in languages other than English classes in Western Australian primary and secondary schools: Theory, practice and perceptions [Doctoral dissertation]. Edith Cowan University.

Tognini, R., & Oliver, R. (2012). L1 use in primary and secondary foreign language classrooms and its contribution to learning. In E. Alcón Soler & M. P. Safont Jordá (eds.), *Discourse and Learning across L2 Instructional Contexts* (pp. 53–78). Amsterdam: Rodopi.

Trofimovich, P., Ammar, A., & Gatbonton, E. (2007) How effective are recasts? The role of attention, memory, and analytical ability. In A. Mackey (ed.),

Conversational Interaction in Second Language Acquisition (pp. 171–195). Oxford: Oxford University Press.

US Department of State (n.d.). Foreign language training: Foreign Service Institute language difficulty categories, www.state.gov/foreign-language-training/ (accessed November 30, 2020).

Valmori, L. (2016). Anxiety in interaction-driven L2 learning [Unpublished PhD dissertation]. Michigan State University.

VanPatten, B., Keating, G., & Wulff, S. (eds.) (2020). *Theories in Second Language Acquisition: An Introduction* (3rd ed.). New York: Routledge.

Varonis, E. M., & Gass, S. (1982). The comprehensibility of non-native speech. *Studies in Second Language Acquisition, 4*(2), 114–136.

Varonis, E. M., & Gass, S. (1985a). Non-native/non-native conversations: A model for negotiation of meaning. *Applied Linguistics, 6*(1), 71–90.

Varonis, E. M., & Gass, S. (1985b). Variation in native speaker speech modification to non-native speakers. *Studies in Second Language Learning, 7*, 35–57.

Vygotsky, L. (1962). *Thought and Language.* Cambridge, MA: MIT Press.

Vygotsky, L. S. (1978). *Mind in Society: The Development of Higher Psychological Processes.* Cambridge, MA: Harvard University Press.

Vygotsky, L. S. (1987). *The Collected Works of L. S. Vygotsky. Vol. 1. Problems of General Psychology.* Including the volume thinking and speech. New York: Plenum Press.

Wagner-Gough, K., & Hatch, E. (1975). The importance of input in second language acquisition studies. *Language Learning, 25,* 297–308.

Wajnryb, R. (1990). *Grammar Dictation.* Oxford: Oxford University Press.

Wesche, M. (1994). Input and interaction in second language acquisition. In C. Gallaway & B. Richards (eds.), *Input and Interaction in Language Acquisition* (pp. 219–249). Cambridge: Cambridge University Press.

Williams, J. N. (1999). Memory, attention, and inductive learning. *Studies in Second Language Acquisition, 21,* 1–48.

Williams, J. N. (2012). Working memory and SLA. In S. Gass & A. Mackey (eds.), *The Routledge Handbook of Second Language Acquisition* (pp. 427–441). New York: Routledge.

Wilson-Duffy, C. (2003). Creating online language activities: Putting task-based language teaching to use (Part 2). *CLEAR News, 7*(2), 1, 3, 6–7.

Wood, D., Bruner, J. S., & Ross, G. (1976). The role of tutoring in problem solving. *Journal of Child Psychology and Psychiatry, 17*(2), 89–100.

Wulff, S. (2013). Input matters: The processor as a statistician. Invited commentary. *Linguistic Approaches to Bilingualism, 3,* 356–360.

Wulff, S. (2021). Usage-based approaches. In N. Tracy-Ventura & M. Paquot (eds.), *Routledge Handbook of SLA and Corpora* (pp. 177–190). New York: Routledge.

Wulff, S., & Ellis, N. C. (2018). Usage-based approaches to second language acquisition. In D. Miller, F. Bayram, J. Rothman, & L. Serratrice (eds.), *Bilingual Cognition and Language: The State of the Science across Its Subfields* (pp. 37–56). Amsterdam/Philadelphia: John Benjamins.

Yang, Y., & Lyster, R. (2010). Effects of form-focused practice and feedback on Chinese EFL learners' acquisition of regular and irregular past tense forms. *Studies in Second Language Acquisition, 32*(2), 235–263.

Yilmaz, Y. (2013). Relative effects of explicit and implicit feedback: The role of working memory capacity and language analytic ability. *Applied Linguistics, 34*, 344–368.

Yilmaz, Y., & Sağdıç, A. (2019). The interaction between inhibitory control and corrective feedback timing. *ITL-International Journal of Applied Linguistics, 170*(2), 204–227.

Ziegler, N. (2016). Synchronous computer-mediated communication and interaction: A meta-analysis. *Studies in Second Language Acquisition, 38*(3), 553–586.

Ziegler, N., & González-Lloret, M. (eds.) (in press). *Handbook of SLA and Technology*. New York: Routledge.

Ziegler, N., & Mackey, A. J. (2017). Interactional feedback in computer-mediated communication: A review and state of the art. In H. Nassaji & E. Kartchava (eds.), *Corrective Feedback in Second Language Teaching and Learning: Research, Theory, Applications, Implications* (pp. 80–94). London: Routledge.

Ziegler, N., Parlak, Ö. , & Phung, H. (in press). Interactionist perspectives and the role of technology in SLA. In N. Ziegler & M. González-Lloret (eds.), *Handbook of SLA and Technology*. New York: Routledge.

Cambridge Elements ≡

Second Language Acquisition

Alessandro Benati

The University of Hong Kong

Alessandro Benati is Director of CAES at The University of Hong Kong (HKU). He is known for his work in second language acquisition and second language teaching. He has published ground-breaking research on the pedagogical framework called Processing Instruction. He is co-editor of a new online series for Cambridge University Press, a member of the REF Panel 2021, and Honorary Professor at York St John University.

John W. Schwieter

Wilfrid Laurier University, Ontario

John W. Schwieter is Associate Professor of Spanish and Linguistics, and Faculty of Arts Teaching Scholar, at Wilfrid Laurier University. His research interests include psycholinguistic and neurolinguistic approaches to multilingualism and language acquisition; second language teaching and learning; translation and cognition; and language, culture, and society.

About the Series

Second Language Acquisition showcases a high-quality set of updatable, concise works that address how learners come to internalize the linguistic system of another language and how they make use of that linguistic system. Contributions reflect the interdisciplinary nature of the field, drawing on theories, hypotheses, and frameworks from education, linguistics, psychology, and neurology, among other disciplines. Each Element in this series addresses several important questions: What are the key concepts?; What are the main branches of research?; What are the implications for SLA?; What are the implications for pedagogy?; What are the new avenues for research?; and What are the key readings?

Cambridge Elements ☰

Second Language Acquisition

Elements in the Series

Proficiency Predictors in Sequential Bilinguals
Lynette Austin, Arturo E. Hernandez and John W. Schwieter

Implicit Language Aptitude
Gisela Granena

Generative Second Language Acquisition
Roumyana Slabakova, Tania Leal, Amber Dudley and Micah Stack

The Acquisition of Aspect in a Second Language
Stefano Rastelli

Focus on Form
Alessandro Benati

Interaction
Jennifer Behney and Susan Gass

A full series listing is available at www.cambridge.org/esla

Printed in the United States
by Baker & Taylor Publisher Services